THE BIG BUSINESS EXECUTIVE

THE
BIG BUSINESS
EXECUTIVE

the factors that made him
1900-1950

---

by MABEL NEWCOMER

NEW YORK AND LONDON

COLUMBIA UNIVERSITY PRESS

ACKNOWLEDGMENTS

MY DEBT to all those who have aided in this study is very great. The big business executives themselves responded generously to my requests to fill in the missing data concerning their careers; and relatives and friends of former executives not only answered questions but often took the trouble to search for information they did not have at hand. Also, in gathering the biographical data, I received invaluable assistance from librarians all over the United States. For these I reserved the most elusive cases, and they rarely failed to supply the missing facts.

For valuable suggestions and criticism on the plan of work and some of the findings, I am indebted to Edna C. Macmahon of the Vassar College Economics Department, who showed a lively interest in the study from its beginning and who read the entire manuscript in the end; and to Arthur H. Cole and other members of the Research Center in Entrepreneurial History at Harvard University, who discussed the study with me while it was in progress.

For assistance in the day-to-day work of the study thanks are due to Barbara Rumpf. She not only assisted in gathering data and tabulating the results, but she also provided invaluable "layman's" criticism. I also wish to express my appreciation of the many ways in which my work was facilitated by the staff of the Vassar College Library and to acknowledge the American Association of University Women Achievement Award, which provided financial assistance for research. Finally, my thanks are due to J. Christopher Herold of the Columbia University Press whose skillful editing has spared the reader a number of obscure statements.

MABEL NEWCOMER

Vassar College
May, 1955

CONTENTS

TABLES

THE BIG BUSINESS EXECUTIVE

CHAPTER ONE

INTRODUCTION

A few, a very few, are exalted to a power which as individuals they could never have wielded. Through the great organizations of which they are the heads, a few are enabled to play a part unprecedented by anything in history in the control of the business operations of the country and in the determination of the happiness of great numbers of people.

WOODROW WILSON

THE economists have long been preoccupied with the problems presented by the growth of the big business corporation. Recognizing the economies of large-scale production on the one hand and the dangers of concentration of power on the other, they have been somewhat ambivalent about the desirability of breaking up the big business unit, whether through strict enforcement of antitrust legislation or by other means. And many have looked toward government regulation rather than prohibition of big business, while others have pointed to the development of "countervailing power," [1] the "corporate conscience," [2] or "professionalization of management" [3] as factors that will preserve the advantages of large-scale production and at the same time prevent the worst evils of monopoly.

One of the economies of big business is found in management. Alfred Marshall lists as the two most important advantages of large-scale production the economy of machinery and the economy of skill.[4] And this last applies, as Marshall himself makes clear, not

The quotation at the head of this chapter is taken from Woodrow Wilson, *The New Freedom,* New York: Doubleday, 1916, p. 6.

[1] J. K. Galbraith, *American Capitalism,* Boston: Houghton Mifflin, 1952.

[2] A. A. Berle, Jr., *The 20th Century Capitalist Revolution,* New York: Harcourt Brace, 1954.

[3] R. A. Gordon, *Business Leadership in the Large Corporation,* Washington: Brookings, 1945.

[4] Alfred Marshall, *Principles of Economics,* 8th ed., London: Macmillan, 1946, p. 278.

merely to the many specialists that the big concern can afford to employ, but more importantly to the opportunity of attracting the ablest executives and using their talents economically. But it cannot be assumed that because the big corporations are in a position to get the best talent to direct them they do so in fact. It can equally well be argued that monopolistic practices may extend to top management itself. The way in which chief executives are chosen in the large corporations and the nature of their jobs are very different from the selection of management and the management function in the small enterprise.

TRENDS IN MANAGEMENT

In the earliest period of big business the leaders were necessarily the founders or builders. They headed the businesses that they had themselves established, either alone or with a small group of associates. And they usually held sufficient stock to guarantee control.

These were followed by the "corporate speculators and plungers" [5] who were at their height around the turn of the century. These bought their offices in the stock market and sold them again in the same market when it proved profitable to do so, or lost them to other plungers if their resources failed to stretch. Some of the more constructive of this group, encouraged by the possibilities offered by New Jersey's new provisions for holding companies, effected combinations and supercombinations from going concerns.[6] The combination movement in the steel industry, culminating in the United States Steel Corporation, is the outstanding instance of this, but Moody lists 318 industrial trusts, 303 of which were formed between 1888 and 1903, and most of them in the last five years of this period. Of these, more than half obtained their charters from New Jersey.[7]

This period was followed by the present era of the "career men" or professionals. There is, of course, no sharp dividing line between these periods. The 1900 generation of this study included a great

[5] The terminology used here follows that used by H. W. Prentis, Jr., in his article, "Liberal Education for Business and Industry," *Bulletin of the American Association of University Professors*, XXXVIII, No. 3 (Autumn, 1952), 346.

[6] The first New Jersey law was passed in 1888 and this was amplified and clarified in succeeding years.

[7] John Moody, *The Truth About the Trusts*, New York: Moody Publishing Company, 1904, pp. 453ff.

many founders, but a number of the railroad executives of this period showed the earmarks of professional administrators even when they represented some outside financial interest. The railroads were, on the average, older than the other groups of corporations, and most of their founders were dead. Also, their period of combination came earlier than that of the industrials, and they had begun to settle down. But the data of this study show a steady decline in the number of founders in all the types of business covered and a corresponding rise in the professional administrators.

Most of the big corporations today have widely scattered stock ownership. This has led, as has often been emphasized, to the separation of ownership and control. The stockholders tend to sign proxies mechanically, since they have little information on which to base considered judgments. Even the directors, who actually elect the top executives, are likely to accept the recommendations of the chief executives themselves without thorough investigation. This results in what Berle and Means have termed "management control." Berle and Means found that 44 percent of their 200 largest corporations (accounting for 58 percent of the assets of the 200) were under management control.[8] And the proportion of large corporations under such control has increased in the past twenty years, partly because of the dissolution of public utility companies under the Public Utility Holding Company Act of 1935, partly because of the decline in nonvoting stock, and partly because of the gradual dispersion of stockholdings in some of the companies the stock of which, when they were younger, was closely held.[9]

No analysis has been made of the control of the 428 corporations included in this study for 1950 that would make it possible to classify them according to the Berle and Means grouping, but a number of individual companies have been found which have moved from one of the other classifications into that of management control, and a study of the stockholdings of the officers indicates that at least three-fourths of the board chairmen and presidents own 1 percent

[8] A. A. Berle, Jr., and G. C. Means, *The Modern Corporation and Private Property*, New York: Commerce Clearing House, 1932, p. 94.

[9] Note the distribution of stock of the Campbell Soup Co. and plans for the distribution of Ford Motor stock (fall of 1954).

or less of the voting stock of their corporations.[10] There have been, of course, some shifts in the other direction. The New York Central Railroad, for instance, which was listed by Berle and Means as under management control, has recently fallen under the control of a minority financial interest directed by Robert C. Young. And Textron now owns approximately 45 percent of American Woolen common.[11] But the general trend is toward increasing management control.

This dispersion of ownership means that the interests and responsibilities of management have shifted. Profits are not the immediate source of the managers' incomes. They are, rather, a mark of professional competence, or perhaps the best assurance of being retained in a high-salaried and respected position. The owners who must be satisfied are likely to be a large number of scattered investors whose interests are not concentrated in a single corporation. Moreover, the growing organization of labor presents another interest to be considered. A satisfied labor force may be as essential to success as satisfied stockholders and satisfied customers. And the "public interest" is growing in recognition. Companies can be found that have representatives of the general public on their boards of directors although they have no representatives either of individual large stockholders or of labor. The Standard Oil Company of New Jersey's Council of Human Relations is a clear recognition of the claims of nonstockholders for consideration by the large corporation. The subdivisions of this council include, along with one for stockholders, departments of employee relations and of public relations, and a government relations counsellor.

The chief executives are professional managers, not entrepreneurs. They may work up within the company or be selected from outside, but they have not initiated the enterprises they head, nor do they own them. They are employees. This does not mean that the modern big business executive necessarily lacks interest in the welfare of the company. On the contrary, as a professional man, he is likely to

[10] Of the 765 officers of the 1950 generation for whom data on stockholdings were found, 83 percent owned 1 percent or less of the stock, but the missing companies include a large proportion of those in which the stock is closely held.

[11] *Wall Street Journal*, August 3, 1954.

take professional pride in "his" company. But the present organization could easily lead to a self-perpetuating management, regardless of the efficiency of the individuals concerned. There is no guarantee that the individuals chosen for the top positions are better executives than many others who might have been found, nor that their interest in the company will lead to the best interests of the stockholders or the final consumers. The chief executive may, for instance, indulge in a relatively unprofitable hobby when all signs point to the fact that better returns might be had from developing a (to him) less glamorous phase of the business. Or he may plow profits back into the company because he wants to see it grow, when the interests of the stockholders would be better served by larger dividends, and the interests of the general public would be furthered by the investment of the earnings elsewhere.

PURPOSE AND SCOPE OF THIS STUDY

There appears to be little popular interest in the chief executives of even our billion-dollar corporations. Their business operations lack the drama of those of the captains of industry of the nineteenth century and the speculators and plungers who succeeded them at the turn of the century. Nor does their mode of living attract attention. The corporations themselves receive a good deal of publicity. But it is only when a corporation executive goes into public life or engages in some activity unrelated to his job that he is likely to emerge as an individual. To illustrate, C. E. Wilson, although he was not ignored when he was president of General Motors, received about ten times as many notices in the *New York Times* in 1953, as Secretary of Defense, as he had in 1950 as president of General Motors. And Robert T. Stevens received just two notices in the *New York Times* in 1950, as board chairman of J. P. Stevens and Company, and more than seventy notices in 1953 as Secretary of the Army. This was before his disagreement with Senator McCarthy had come to public attention.

With a few exceptions, the executives themselves tend to encourage, or at least to accept, this impersonal attitude. It is not that many are seeking anonymity. In the course of this study the writer has had occasion to request personal data from a large number of the officials included in the study, and very few have failed to comply with the request. But neither do they appear to seek publicity. Important business decisions tend to be reported as actions of the corporations rather than of their officials. Sometimes news comes from an unnamed "spokesman" of the company. In short, the actions of these officials suggest that they regard themselves more as trustees or responsible public servants than as dictators or important men of power.

But while popular interest in these executives appears to lag, the changes in the rights and duties of management that have come with the growth in size of the corporations and with the dispersion of ownership have led to renewed interest, on the part of the social scientists, both in the executive function and in the origins of the executives themselves. Most of the studies in this field have concerned the nature of the executive function, but several deal with the social origins of groups of business leaders, both early and contemporary.[12] Very little study has been made, however, of the total business experience and training of the individuals who reach the top executive positions or how this is changing. What are the qualifications of these individuals in terms of education and experience? Is this training and experience what would be expected in the light of demands of the job itself? Does it differ for different fields of business and for corporations of different sizes? By what route did these men reach the top position in our largest corporations? To what extent is free entry still possible in big business? How many aspirants

[12] The most extensive early study in this field is F. W. Taussig and C. S. Joslyn, *American Business Leaders*, New York: Macmillan, 1932. More recent studies include William Miller, ed., *Men in Business*, Cambridge: Harvard University Press, 1952; T. C. Cochran, *Railroad Leaders, 1845–1890*, Cambridge: Harvard University Press, 1953; Suzanne I. Keller, "The Social Origins and Career Lines of Three Generations of American Business Leaders," New York: Columbia University, 1953 (Ph.D. thesis, unpublished); Mabel Newcomer, "The Chief Executives of Large Business Corporations," in *Explorations in Entrepreneurial History*, V (Harvard University, 1952–53), 1–33; and the following articles in the *Journal of Economic History:* William Miller, "American Historians and the Business Elite," IX, No. 2 (November, 1949), 184–208; C. Wright Mills, "The American Business Elite: a Collective Portrait," Supplement V (1945), 20–44; C. M. Destler, "Entrepreneurial Leadership Among the 'Robber Barons,'" Supplement VI (1946), 28–49. Also, "More Facts About Presidents," *The Corporate Director* (November, 1950), and "The Nine Hundred," *Fortune*, XLVI, No. 5 (November, 1952), 132ff.

can start a new concern? And has the economy of skill that Marshall claimed for big business been realized? Does the competitive mechanism operate to select the best-qualified candidates in the well-established companies? Or do seniority, chance, and family influence play more important roles in the final selection?

It is on such questions as these that this study attempts to shed some light. The data presented here are concerned with the way in which top management of the largest corporations is selected, and even more with the training, experience, and family background of the chief executives, and how they rose to the top. Three "generations" of executives have been included, covering the period 1898 to 1953, in order to trace any changes in the kind of men selected as the nature of the job has changed.

PERIODS COVERED

The three periods selected were designed to include the current group of executives and the two preceding generations, in order to measure changes in the training and experience from one generation to the next. It was assumed that twenty-five years was a sufficient period of time to get an almost completely new group of executives. This proved to be the case in spite of the fact that in the end the time span used for each generation left only about twenty years between generations. The 1900 group actually covers executives holding office any time during the five years 1899 to 1903 inclusive. The 1925 group covers those holding office in the three years 1923 to 1925 inclusive. And the 1950 group includes those holding office in the period from January 1, 1948 to June 30, 1953.[13] Only 19 of the 1,900 officers appear again in the 1925 group. This is about 6 percent of either group. And 33 of the 1925 group reappear in the 1950 group. This amounts to 10 percent of the 1925 group and 4 percent of the larger 1950 group. None is included in all three periods, but a few of the 1950 officers had held office more than fifty years.

Although the periods were chosen without reference to business

[13] The shorter middle period was used merely to keep the number of cases smaller. This shorter period produced as many executives as the longer period for 1900.

conditions, all three periods have some important factors in common. All are periods of rather exceptional prosperity following on war, although the war preceding the first period was too limited and short to affect business as profoundly as World Wars I and II. All three periods were likewise periods of active business combination. The first period, however, as has already been indicated, was one in which a much larger sector of big business was affected by the combination movement than in the later periods. Also it was characterized by a kind of financial manipulation that would hardly be tolerated today.

The most important difference in the three periods is probably in the age of the business concerns themselves. In 1900 they were younger than in the later periods. In many instances their founders still controlled them and there had been little opportunity for a top executive either to work up within the company or to inherit it. This makes an important difference in the type of executive found.

Another important difference between the earliest and latest periods is the extent of government control. The Sherman Antitrust Act and the Interstate Commerce Commission existed in 1900 but they had not yet shown their strength. The Public Utility Holding Company Act and the Securities and Exchange Commission came much later. Also, the growing dispersion of stock ownership, the increase in self-financing, and a shift in public attitudes toward big business which goes farther than the laws have all had their effect on management. These differences are reflected in the statistics concerning the executives in office—their training, their terms of office, and how they got to the top.

CORPORATIONS INCLUDED

The corporations selected for this study are the largest railroad, public utility, and industrial corporations in each of the three periods. Financial corporations were excluded because it was necessary to limit either the areas of business activity or the number of corporations in each field. The more thoroughgoing study in the more limited field was decided on, leaving the financial corporations for possible later exploration. The grouping of corporations in the three types of business included follows for the most part that found in *Moody's*

Manuals of Investments. In consequence, steamship and air lines are included with industrials, and the public utility group consists mainly of power, street railway, and telephone and telegraph companies.[14] Industrials also include mercantile companies, but the majority are manufactures.

The corporations within these groups are the large ones. For 1950 all corporations with assets in excess of $75,000,000, as listed in the 1950 *Moody's Manuals,* were included, with the exception of subsidiaries of corporations in the sample. Thus the Standard Oil Company of New Jersey is included, but not the Humble Oil and Refining Company, although the latter had assets in excess of $800,000,000 in 1950. The classification as subsidiaries follows that found in Moody. In addition, a scattering of smaller companies was taken. Most of these had assets in excess of $50,000,000.[15] Also, such corporations as could be found that were not included in Moody but which had assets in excess of $75,000,000 (e.g., the Lykes Brothers Steamship Co.) have been included. This is a very small group.

The same procedure was followed for 1925 and 1900, except that the asset limit above which all corporations were included is smaller —$50,000,000 in 1925 and $25,000,000 in 1900. These limits are roughly comparable in terms of purchasing power of the dollar in each of the three periods, measured by the Bureau of Labor Statistics index of wholesale prices. In the earlier periods, too, a sample of smaller corporations has been included. Also, in the earliest group, large corporations formed in the three years following 1900 have been included.

In view of the extensive combination movement that occurred in this early period, accompanied by generous stock watering in

[14] The only departures from the Moody classification are to include the Greyhound Corporation, with air and water transportation, in "industrials" and to include broadcasting companies with public utilities. The number of corporations whose classification is somewhat arbitrary is comparatively small.

[15] Those, eight in all, with even smaller assets were relatively large companies that had been included in the 1925 sample but which, though still large, did not have assets of $50,000,000 in 1950. An attempt was made in selecting the group with assets under $75,000,000 to give reasonable representation to each field of enterprise, and within the industrial group to distribute the cases among heavy and light industry and mercantile firms. Since, however, size is related to the field of activity, this group contains a relatively higher proportion of light industry and mercantile enterprises than the larger groups and relatively fewer railroads and public utilities.

many cases, and of the fact that there was a greater measure of privacy concerning financing than in more recent years, assets are a very unsatisfactory measure of size. However, no better measure appears to be available.[16] In general, those corporations that grew to foremost rank in the first decade of this century were included in the early group, but their assets as of 1900 (or the first year of their organization for those formed after 1900) have been used in the classification according to size.

The corporations included in the sample held a large proportion of all business assets in each period studied. No exact figures are available, but the ratio of the total reported assets of the corporations in the sample for each of the three periods to estimated business wealth in the one year in each period for which such estimates are available shows that 1900 assets amounted to 49.9 percent of business wealth, 1925 assets to 32.1 percent, and 1950 assets to 40.0 percent.[17] There is some double counting in the asset figures, and there is considerable overvaluation of assets in 1900. Also, the asset figure for 1950 is two years later than the figure for wealth. On the other hand, the figures for business wealth include some nonbusiness categories, and the corporation assets do not include all the assets of partially owned subsidiaries. It is the writer's guess that the corporations in the 1950 sample include at least one-third of business assets and the earlier ones a little less.

[16] Gross receipts were the test used in Taussig and Joslyn, *American Business Leaders,* but these vary so much from one year to the next that they leave much to the chance of the specific year chosen. The gross receipts of United States Steel, e.g., in 1932 were one-fourth of what they had been in 1929, but United States Steel continued to be a very large corporation.

[17] The figure for business wealth includes private nonfarm land, nonresidential and mining structures, producer durables, and nonfarm inventories as reported in the National Bureau of Economic Research, *Studies in Income and Wealth,* XIV (1951), 18. The years used are 1900, 1924, and 1948. These do not correspond precisely to the years for which assets were obtained. Moreover, the items included in business wealth cover a somewhat wider category. And finally, the asset figures are not accurate valuations. They do not include much double counting, however, since the sample omits subsidiaries. The 1900 figure is doubtless excessive in view of the overvaluation of assets in this period. The computation is as follows (in billion dollars):

	1900	1924	1948
Total business wealth	34.5	151.9	305.4
Total wealth	81.1	352.5	797.0
Assets of sample corporations	17.2	48.8	122.2
Percent of business wealth	49.8	32.1	40.0
Percent of total wealth	21.1	13.8	15.3

The age of the corporation, as well as the size, is an important factor influencing the choice of top executives. Most of the corporations of 1900 were ten years old or less, whereas most of the 1950 corporations were more than fifty years old. The age has been measured, not by the year in which the charter was obtained, but by the year in which the business was started, whether as an individual enterprise, partnership, or corporation. In the case of mergers of existing companies (and practically all the large corporations have at some time formed combinations of existing companies) the decision as to the date of origin was necessarily somewhat arbitrary. In general, if the merger was that of a large company with one or more small ones, the age of the large company was the one used. If, however, the combination included a large number of companies, no one of which was dominant in size, it was accepted as a new business, and its age was measured by the year of combination.

While more than half of the 1950 corporations were in existence in 1900, according to this classification of age, only 99 of them were included in the 1900 corporations. The rest were too small. Ninety-three more of the 1950 corporations were included in the 1925 group, and 236 appear only in the 1950 group. Most of the corporations included in the earlier periods that do not appear in the 1950 sample have been merged with other companies as comparatively small subdivisions. Forty-eight continued to exist but did not grow enough to be continued in the later samples, 20 were liquidated completely (most of them in the period between 1900 and 1925), and 7 public utilities were transferred to municipal ownership. This is a demonstration of the stability and growth of big business in this period.

The number of corporations for each type of business is given in Tables 1 and 2, both for different asset sizes and for different ages.

OFFICES INCLUDED AND DATA FOR EACH OFFICER

The offices selected are those of the president and board chairman. The status and duties of these two officials differ from one corporation to another. Most of the textbooks describe the chairmanship as primarily an advisory position. To illustrate, Gerstenberg states that the chairman "is the Nestor of the company. His advice is needed in questions of policy and in matters of great importance. His position corresponds to that of senior partner of the firm." The president, in contrast, is "the managing director." [18] And it is still common practice for the president to be promoted to the board chairmanship, and sometimes to semiretirement along with it.

TABLE 1

NUMBER AND SIZE OF CORPORATIONS IN SAMPLE

ASSETS IN MILLIONS OF DOLLARS	NUMBER OF CORPORATIONS			
	Railroad	*Public Utility*	*Industrial*	*Total*
1900				
40 and under [a]	12	26	58	96
41–100	25	14	35	74
Over 100	28	6	10	44
Total	65	46	103	214
1925				
80 and under [b]	5	23	69	97
81–250	14	20	56	90
Over 250	25	5	21	51
Total	44	48	146	238
1950				
100 and under [c]	8	21	106	135
101–200	8	38	85	131
201–500	14	32	54	100
Over 500	16	18	28	62
Total	46	109	273	428

YEAR	MEDIAN ASSETS IN MILLIONS OF DOLLARS			
1900	89	35	36	45
1925	307	93	83	97
1950	305	189	125	147

[a] Includes all companies with assets in excess of $25,000,000—60 in all; and 36 companies with assets below this figure.

[b] Includes all companies with assets in excess of $50,000,000—51 in all; and 46 with assets below this figure.

[c] Includes all companies with assets in excess of $75,000,000—84 in all; and 51 with assets below this figure.

But increasingly in the big corporation these offices represent two full-time positions. Chairmen sometimes become presidents as well as vice versa, and either may be the chief executive officer. The title

[18] C. W. Gerstenberg, *Financial Organization and Management of Business*, 2d rev. ed., New York: Prentice Hall, 1939, pp. 94–95.

of chief executive officer sometimes moves with the individual from one office to the other. In announcing changes in either the presidency or the chairmanship, it is increasingly customary to specify which incumbent is the chief executive officer. Thus it is necessary, in order to include the top officials, to include both offices. Actually,

TABLE 2

AGE OF CORPORATIONS [a]

Age [a]	Railroad	Public Utility	Industrial	Total
1900				
Over 50 years	19	1	2	22
21–50	24	6	11	41
11–20	15	12	10	37
10 and under	7	27	80	114
Total	65	46	103	214
1925				
Over 50 years	31	7	30	68
21–50	11	25	89	125
11–20	2	13	17	32
10 and under	. . .	3	10	13
Total	44	48	146	238
1950				
Over 50 years	42	30	146	218
21–50	4	72	119	195
11–20	. . .	2	7	9
10 and under	. . .	5 [b]	1 [c]	6
Total	46	109	273	428

[a] As of 1900, 1925, and 1950 respectively, for the three groups.
[b] Natural gas companies.
[c] Kaiser-Frazer.

the only measurable difference found in the holders of these two offices is that the chairmen are on the average a little older than the presidents. This is true whether or not the chairmanship is preceded by the presidency.

The number of offices and officers are listed in Table 3. In the analysis of the characteristics of these officers which follows, those holding more than one presidency or chairmanship have been counted for each office held. Since the number of these is small, and since in most cases it is the characteristics of the holder of a specific office that are important, no attempt has been made to eliminate this double counting.[19]

TABLE 3

Number of Corporations, Officers, and Offices [a]

	1900	1925	1950
Corporations	214	238	428
Officers	284	319 [b]	863
Offices	316	330	882

[a] Since some individuals have held the presidency or board chairmanship of more than one corporation, the number of offices exceeds the number of officers.

[b] Including 19 officers who were also in the 1900 sample and 33 who were also in the 1950 sample.

The following information was sought for each of these officers:

1. Name of officer and office held
2. Company: name, assets, and year of organization
3. Year and country of birth
4. Father's occupation and family status, i.e., wealthy, middle income, or poor
5. Education: grammar school, high school, college
6. Academic degrees, and institution attended
7. Political and religious affiliations
8. Job history
   a. Family influence in obtaining first full-time position
   b. Nature of first full-time position and age of beginning
   c. Other positions prior to work with company of which he became chief executive
   d. Principal occupation or profession
   e. Government service
   f. History with company, i.e., number of years before becoming chief executive, and office and department prior to reaching top position
9. History as president or board chairman
   a. How position was obtained

[19] Our concern is, e.g., with the age at which the office was first attained. Thus a president of two corporations may have achieved the first presidency at 50 and the second at 60. Also, it is more important to know how many corporations are manned with college graduates than to know how many individuals in top positions have college degrees.

b. Age at which first appointed

c. Length of service in top position

d. Reasons for termination of service

e. Stockholdings and compensation

f. Number of outside directorships

In addition to the data concerning chief executives, a sample was taken of the size of boards of directors, the principal occupations of board members, and the number of interlocking directorates. Since the entire board of directors has the ultimate authority to select the chief executives, it has seemed important to know something about the composition of these boards. The data on directors' occupations are limited to the recent period.

All the data have been analyzed for each period by the type and size of corporation, and the officers of each period have also been tabulated in two groups according to the length of time they had held office as of 1900, 1925, and 1950 respectively. Since the long periods of office for many of the executives tend to blur the changes from one period to the next, the separate tabulation of the more recent appointees sometimes makes the trends clearer. The time of appointment rather than the age of the individual was selected for this subdivision of data, since it seems more important to know what the differences in training are for the individuals appointed in any two periods than to know the differences in training for those born in any two periods. Not all of this detail is presented here, since much of it showed no important contrasts.

SOURCES

The sources of information concerning these individuals are too many and too diverse to list. The reference works found most useful are *Who's Who in America, National Cyclopaedia of American Biography, Dictionary of American Biography, Current Biography,* and newspaper obituaries, particularly those in the *New York Times.* These have been supplemented by published genealogies, local histories, and a large number of volumes of biography for special regions. When these sources had been exhausted, letters were sent to all living officers for whom important data were missing. For those no longer living, requests were sent to relatives when these could be found, and to corporations. For the older groups, census records were found useful for fathers' occupations, and sometimes for family status, since the value of homes or farms was given. And last but not least, the librarians of the home-town public libraries proved a mine of information. In consequence, it has been possible to obtain better than 95 percent returns for the items that were regarded as most important. Occasionally conflicting information was found, but in these cases it was usually possible to verify the information. For the most part the sources were so limited that it was necessary to take the information given without further check of any kind. No attempt was made to go beyond the printed record for such items as religious and political affiliations, compensation, and stock holdings,[20] in the belief that requests for too many items would result in more frequent failure to give any information and in the consequent risk of obtaining a biased sample for the most important items.

LIMITATIONS OF THE STUDY

A statistical study, however complete the returns and however representative the sample (and for the largest corporations the "sample" is one hundred percent), cannot by its nature give any definitive answer to the important questions: Why was this particular man chosen for this particular job? Was his training and experience especially appropriate for the demands of the position? How wide a search was made to find the best person for this important post? Is it better to select men from within the organization for the top positions, or are broader contacts and experience more important than knowledge of the peculiar problems of the corporation in question? Is the method of selection better or worse than it was fifty years ago? And are the executives today an abler group than those of the earlier period? However, the factual data can provide a starting point for obtaining answers to such questions. And some attempt has been made to relate the findings to current discussions of the nature of the executive function and the best qualifications for high office.

[20] These last two items were obtained from individual company notices of stockholders' meetings.

CHAPTER TWO

THE NATURE OF
THE EXECUTIVE FUNCTION
IN THE
BIG CORPORATION

Whatever his title, the chief executive in our largest corporations is not ordinarily the type of creative and aggressive business leader who is both famous and infamous in the annals of American industry. He is not the restless dynamic individual of an earlier generation who, owning his company, pioneered into new lines and "risked his shirt" building up a new business organization. Rather, he is a professional executive doing a "management" job—co-ordinating his firm's activities, approving decisions that flow up to him from his subordinates, but doing less and less initiation.

R. A. GORDON

BEFORE turning to the data concerning the individual officers, it should be useful to review the procedure by which they are elected to office, to describe briefly the nature of the job and what are generally considered to be the most important qualifications for it, and to indicate the distribution of powers between the president and board chairman and between the executives and their boards of directors.

The president and board chairman are elected by the entire board of directors, and the directors in turn are elected by the stockholders. The stockholders do not vote directly for these officers, and it seems doubtful if the majority of small stockholders in our giant corporations could even name the president or board chairman of the corporations whose stock they own, in spite of the fact that communica-

The quotation at the head of this chapter is taken from R. A. Gordon, *Business Leadership in the Large Corporation,* Washington: Brookings, 1945, p. 71.

tions to scattered stockholders are more and more frequent and color-ful, and invitations to attend stockholders' meetings in person, with free lunch provided, are increasingly cordial.

In practice, it appears to be customary for the outgoing president —or chief executive officer—to name his own successor, even though he may have no important investment in the company. This does not mean that the directors have abdicated their authority. It is rather an expression of their continued confidence in the chief executive's judgment. And the chief executive, in making his recommendations, doubtless takes into consideration the probable acceptability of the candidate to the directors and other officers. There are, to be sure, well-known instances of the outgoing officer's wishes being ignored. Nevertheless the practice described above is widespread, and it appears to perpetuate, for better or for worse, the policies of the existing administration, since the executive is apt to select those who see eye to eye with him.

The job of the executive in the big business organization is, first, to formulate long-range policies and to make important decisions and accept responsibility for them. "Management does not do things. It decides what should be done." [1] And second, his job is to keep the organization running smoothly from day to day. "The job of professional management . . . is to conduct the affairs of the enterprise in its charge in such a way as to maintain an equitable and workable balance among the claims of the various directly interested groups . . . the stockholders, employees, customers, and the public at large." [2]

As a corollary of this, the chief executive normally has the right to appoint the second-ranking officers with whom he must work directly. This requires the ability to judge other people's qualifications for their jobs, since he must depend on the other officers both for information on which to base his decisions and for the execution of his policies. It also requires the ability to work successfully with people. This quality is increasingly emphasized in the discussions of what kind of individual will succeed at the job and what kind of

[1] P. F. Drucker, The New Society, New York: Harper, 1950, p. 204.
[2] F. W. Abrams, "Management's Responsibilities in a Complex World," Harvard Business Review, XXIX, No. 3 (May, 1951), 29–30.

training he should have. "The role of the administrator seems destined to become more and more that of the instructor—the kind of teacher who understands his pupils, accepts their differences, commands their respect, and inspires them to creative work of every kind." [3]

And finally, corporation presidents, no less than university presidents, are expected to participate in the field of public affairs—whether in an advisory capacity on some national commission or committee or merely as active members of their home communities. "High executives are increasingly called upon to act outside the organization, on its behalf, with respect to affairs of the larger community." [4] The Young Presidents' Organization, in recognition of these demands, urges its members to take an active part in hometown politics. [5] And the corporation officials themselves, for all their complaints concerning government interference, show an increasing awareness of a public responsibility that was scarcely dreamed of in the earlier period.

All this points to the fact that detailed knowledge of production techniques, financing, and marketing must, in the big corporation, be left to others—staffs of specialists with which the big corporation is ordinarily well equipped. "As chairman, I don't pretend really to know what the research people are doing; it's my job to keep them going in harmonious balance with the rest of the outfit." [6] What is needed is someone who can formulate general policies, make the necessary decisions, and take full responsibility for them; and someone who can implement his policies through his ability to select the right kind of officers and get them to work together harmoniously in carrying out the program. "The higher the positions in the line of authority, the more general the abilities required." [7] But little guidance has been found as to how this kind of ability can be dis-

[3] A. T. Collier, "Business Leadership and a Creative Society," *Harvard Business Review*, XXXI, No. 1 (January–February, 1953), 37.

[4] L. H. Jenks, "Role Structure of Entrepreneurial Personality," in *Change and the Entrepreneur*, Cambridge: Harvard University Press, 1949, p. 111.

[5] *New York Times*, April 5, 1953.

[6] Corporation board chairman quoted in F. L. Allen, *The Big Change*, New York: Harper, 1952, p. 251.

[7] C. I. Barnard, *The Functions of the Executive*, Cambridge: Harvard University Press, 1948, p. 222.

covered or created. "We deliberately and more and more turn out specialists; but we do not develop general executives well by specific efforts, and we know very little about how to do it." [8]

This description applies particularly to the chief executive of our large business corporation today. The requirements for the executive of 1900 were somewhat different. Power was more often concentrated in the hands of a single individual then than now, and consequently a more aggressive and ruthless type of leadership than is acceptable today was likely to succeed. The change is due to many developments. The corporations today are older and more firmly established. And financial control is less concentrated. But even the executive who has organized his own corporation and owns a controlling share of the stock must reckon with strong labor unions, whereas the 1900 leader was usually able to ignore them. And he faces more extensive government controls and a changed public opinion which has a subtle but far-reaching influence.

The foregoing discussion concerns the job and qualifications of the chief executive officer, whatever his title. Most frequently he is the president, but the board chairman often holds this position, and on rare occasions some other officer, perhaps the executive vice president, is the chief executive officer. But regardless of whether the president or the board chairman holds the position of chief executive officer, there is no clear division of functions between the two offices. The president may be in almost complete control or he may be the board chairman's errand boy. Or there may be a division of powers and responsibilities that leaves the outsider in doubt as to who is the superior officer. And finally, the two officers may work so closely together that any decision made and any action taken may in fact be a joint action or decision.

Group action is increasingly frequent. And the group may extend beyond the two chief officers to the executive committee or even the entire board. This last is probably true only in those corporations where the board is made up exclusively of officers, but in these there is a good deal of evidence that the entire group participates actively in all important decisions.

[8] *Ibid.*

This, too, is in contrast to the situation in 1900, when the board chairman, in those cases where this office was not merged with that of the presidency, was usually remote from day-to-day administration—a banker with an important financial interest, perhaps, or a semiretired former president. The board of directors, too, was less often an active and well-informed group of men in the earlier period, although the inside board was not unknown.

In summary, the executive function is no longer wielded by dictators. It requires leaders who can cooperate and persuade. "Hearst was the very last of the nineteenth-century style of monolithic individualists," [9] and "such autocrats as the late table-pounding George Washington Hill of American Tobacco and the rambunctious Sewell Avery of Montgomery Ward are in increasingly short supply." [10] At this writing even Sewell Avery's control has been seriously challenged.[11]

[9] S. H. Holbrook, *The Age of the Moguls,* New York: Doubleday, 1953, p. 319.
[10] F. L. Allen, *The Big Change,* p. 250.
[11] *The Wall Street Journal,* August 27, 1954.

CHAPTER THREE

THE BOARD OF DIRECTORS

The Board is indisputably the core of the management of the company. Its decisions are group decisions. . . . It seems likely, the members being only human, that the views of the Chairman and the President carry more weight than those of ordinary members; but this . . . does not give either domination of the Board.

C. HARTLEY GRATTAN

THE president of the corporation is quite regularly a member of the board. He frequently serves, even in the larger corporations, in the dual capacity of president and board chairman. And if he is the chief executive officer, he is likely to be the dominating member of the board even though he is not also chairman. Nevertheless, the board shares the powers and responsibilities of top management. In fact, it holds the ultimate power and responsibility. It is, therefore, important to consider the size and composition of the board and such changes as have taken place in these over the past fifty years, since the kind of board is bound to influence the kind of chief executives chosen as the leaders of big business.

This study of the size and composition of the boards of directors is based largely on the data in *Moody's Manuals.* The tabulation of specific occupations for the 1952 boards, however, is from individual company notices of stockholders meetings.

SIZE OF THE BOARD

The size of the board varies with the kind of corporation, the median for the corporations included in this study being 14 for railroads, 12 for industrials, and 9 for public utilities in 1949. For all

The quotation at the head of this chapter is taken from F. L. Allen, *The Big Change,* New York: Harper, 1952, p. 251.

corporations combined it was 12. Except for the railroads, with a median board of 13 in 1900, the median for each of these groups was the same in 1900 as it was in 1949. There appears to be no trend toward either larger or smaller boards. The range, in 1949, was from 3 to 34, but more than half of the boards were within the range of 9 to 15 both in 1949 and 1900.

Among the industrial corporations there is some tendency for board membership to increase with size. The median membership for corporations with assets in excess of $200,000,000 in 1949 was 15. This appears to be the result of an attempt to give representation to the management of underlying companies where consolidations have been effected—either as part of the bargain or in the interests of good morale rather than in recognition of any real need for a larger or more varied board in the larger corporations. Numerous instances of such increased representation at the time of consolidation have been found. Yet two-fifths of the larger corporations of this study—including some of the largest—have from nine to twelve directors. In the billion-dollar class, Gulf Oil Corporation had ten directors in 1949 and only nine in 1953. Several of the largest oil companies have ten to twelve directors. And the public utilities, with average assets in excess of the industrials, typically have a board of nine.

COMPOSITION OF THE BOARD

The composition of the board of directors varies with the type of business. Also, it has changed during the period covered in this study. The factor of greatest interest in considering the relation of the board to the chief executive is, probably, the proportion of members who are full-time employees of the corporation. The president is almost always a member of the board and, of course, a full-time employee. And the board chairman is usually a full-time employee, although there are some exceptions. This position is frequently filled by the president himself. In 1900 only about one corporation in ten listed a chairman of the board who was not also the president. In 1949 nearly half of the corporations listed both a chairman and a president, and among the industrials a substantial majority have both a chairman and a president.[1] Even when the two offices are separate, however, the majority of chairmen are full-time—or nearly full-time—employees of their companies. This is indicated by the salaries paid. Only 34 chairmen have been found among those included in this study who receive no regular salary.[2] Over four-fifths receive more than $25,000 in compensation, and the median salary is approximately the same as that for the presidents.

The proportion of board members recruited from officers of the company, as reported in *Moody's Manual*, is given in Table 4 for 1900 and 1949. A check with data concerning the principal occupations of directors found in the individual company notices of stockholders' meetings shows that the Moody data do not include all active officers. A tabulation of 170 companies from the notices for 1952, also given in Table 4, shows no important differences in the proportion of officers, as listed in these two sources, for the railroads and public utilities, but the company notices show a much larger proportion of officers for the industrial corporations than was found for these in *Moody's Manual*. While the sample taken from the company notices includes only two-fifths of the corporations used in this study, a comparison of the data in the two sources for a number of individual corporations indicates that the difference is due to the incompleteness of the list of officers reported in *Moody's Manual* rather than to any bias in the selection of the sample.[3]

For the industrial corporations, the data from the company notices show 55 percent of the companies with half or more of the board made up of active or retired officers, as compared with 39 percent of the 1949 Moody data. The percentage of total board members in the 1952 group who are active officers is 54, with 3 percent more recruited from retired officers. The inclusion of the retired officers

[1] These data apply only to the large corporations included in this study. Smaller corporations have one man holding both offices with greater frequency.

[2] Salary data were found for 87 percent of the chairmen in this study. They are for the year 1952, except for those chairmen retiring before this year or appointed since.

[3] Some bias might arise from the fact that the corporations that do not publish these data in notices of stockholders' meetings tend to be the smaller and more closely held companies. The number of these is, however, comparatively small.

in the 1952 data accounts, therefore, for only a small part of the difference between the two sources. The trend indicated by the Moody data as between 1900 and 1949 appears to reflect a genuine trend, however. While the Moody data understate the number of inside board members, there is no indication that this understatement is greater in one of the years than in the other.

TABLE 4

PROPORTION OF COMPANY OFFICERS SERVING ON BOARDS OF DIRECTORS, 1900, 1949, AND 1952 [a]

Percentage of Officers on Board	All Corporations	Railroads	Public Utilities	Industrials
1900				
Under 50	92.7	98.8	90.0	86.1
50–99	6.3	1.2	10.0	11.4
100	1.0	. . .	. . .	2.5
	100.0	100.0	100.0	100.0
1949				
Under 50	72.1	95.8	88.1	61.4
50–99	27.7	4.2	11.9	38.3
100	0.2	. . .	. . .	0.3
	100.0	100.0	100.0	100.0
1952				
Under 50	66.5	100.0	89.8	44.7
50–99	25.8	. . .	10.2	41.5
100	7.7	. . .	. . .	13.8
	100.0	100.0	100.0	100.0

[a] The data for 1900 and 1949 have been compiled from *Moody's Manuals* and are comparable as far as can be ascertained. The 1952 data have been compiled from *Notices of Annual Meetings of Stockholders*, and these give a more complete record of officers than is found in *Moody's Manuals*. Consequently, the differences between 1949 and 1952 are due to the more complete record of officers in the *Notices* rather than to any trend or the fact that the 1952 data comprise a smaller number of corporations. The 1952 sample includes 27 railroads, 49 public utilities, and 94 industrials. The 1949 data include all the corporations whose presidents and chairmen have been included in this study, with the exception of a small number for which data were not included in *Moody's Manuals*.

Table 5 shows the proportion of the total number of directors in different types of business who were active officers of the company. Both these tables show a trend toward a larger proportion of officers, but particularly among the industrial companies. This trend is reversed for the railroads, with only 17 percent of their board members recruited from officers in 1949, as compared with 22 percent in 1900.

TABLE 5

OFFICERS SERVING ON BOARDS OF DIRECTORS, 1900 AND 1949 [a]

	1900			1949		
	Number of Directors	Number of Officers	Percentage of Officers	Number of Directors	Number of Officers	Percentage of Officers
Railroad	972	210	21.6	646	110	17.0
Public utility	312	80	25.6	1,354	420	31.0
Industrial	947	284	30.0	3,703	1,595	43.1
Total	2,231	574	25.7	5,703	2,125	37.3

[a] Data compiled from *Moody's Manuals.*

TABLE 6

CORPORATION OFFICES REPRESENTED ON BOARDS OF DIRECTORS, 1900 AND 1949 [a]

(*Percentages of different ranks*)

OFFICE	ALL CORPORATIONS		RAILROADS		PUBLIC UTILITIES		INDUSTRIALS	
	1900	1949	1900	1949	1900	1949	1900	1949
President [b]	33.3	22.0	39.0	43.6	37.5	29.0	27.9	18.6
Chairman [c]	3.3	10.6	5.2	14.5	—	10.5	2.8	10.4
Vice president [d]	38.9	55.5	39.1	25.4	37.5	51.5	39.2	58.5
Other	24.4	11.9	16.7	16.4	25.0	9.0	30.0	12.5
	100.0	100.0	100.0	100.0	100.0	100.0	100.0	100.0

[a] Data compiled from *Moody's Manuals.*
[b] Including president-chairmen.
[c] Excluding president-chairmen.
[d] Executive vice presidents and first vice presidents account for 4.7 percent of board officers in 1900 and 7.3 percent in 1949.

Table 6 shows the proportions of officers recruited from different offices. The percentage of presidents among the officer members of the board has declined from one-third to less than one-fourth, and vice presidents outnumber all other officers combined. The rise in vice presidents and the decline in other second-ranking officers is not so much a reflection of differences in the kind of talent recruited for the boards as a growing tendency to confer the title of vice president on those serving in such positions as secretaries, treasurers, and general managers.

The large proportion of the board membership recruited from officers—half or more in the majority of industrial corporations— raises many interesting questions. The board determines the broad general policies under which the executives operate. Moreover, the board elects the chief executives and fixes their salaries. This form of organization was presumably designed to provide a check on executive powers, which is greatly diminished when the majority of board members are the same executive officers who are subject to board control. As Gordon notes, the "board as an independent supervisory body has ceased to exist." [4] While it is still possible for the stockholders to overrule the board in really important matters, or to fail to reelect them, this is no substitute for the better informed and continuous watchfulness of a board which meets at frequent intervals, hears reports, asks pertinent questions, and reaches reasonably informed judgments. Moreover, in a corporation where stock is widely distributed, the possibility of dissatisfied stockholders mustering the necessary votes to force a change is very slim. It is easier to sell the stock. The cost alone is prohibitive, as was made abundantly clear in the recent New York Central upset. The cost of this proxy battle was estimated to be more than one million dollars.[5] Only when the dissatisfied minority has really important holdings, as in the case of the New York Central, is the chance of getting a new deal a real one.

Also, quite aside from the check provided by a board of outsiders, there is often need for the perspective that those less involved in the day to day problems of administration can provide; and perhaps for specialized knowledge not available among the officers. And "connections" with other kinds of business, e.g., the banker, lawyer, customer, or supplier of goods and services, may be important. Finally, the large but comparatively inactive stockholders, where these exist, have special claims to membership on the board.

The majority of those writing on this subject favors the board

[4] R. A. Gordon, *Business Leadership in the Large Corporation*, Washington: Brookings, 1945, p. 120.

[5] *Fortune*, L, No. 2 (August, 1954), 87.

with a minority representation from the company's own officers. Gerard Swope, for example, expresses a preference for a board (like that of his General Electric Corporation) made up largely of outsiders.[6] Sidney Weinberg also favors such a board. He says, "I believe the ideal board should have a majority of its members chosen from outside the management and a minority from the executive officers group, although I am on many boards that do not have this ratio.[7] Weinberg held more directorships in the large corporations included in this study in 1949 than any other individual.

Some corporations with inside boards have, from time to time, modified their policy, whether from uneasy consciences or from stockholder pressure. The American Smelting and Refining Company yielded to the pressure of minority stockholders in 1922 and elected a substantial number of outsiders to the board.[8] The new directors were, however, nominated by the Guggenheims. This company still has outsiders on the board, but these constitute a minority. The P. Lorillard Company submitted a resolution in their 1943 proxy statement to the effect that at least six members of the board shall be nominated from outsiders, explaining that the board should be free of any management domination.[9] However, the 1953 Lorillard board contained only three such outsiders. And the Socony-Vacuum Oil Company has recently added a representative of the general public, the president of Columbia University, to an otherwise totally inside board. These are, however, exceptions. No support is found in the statistics for Gilbert's contention that the inside board is becoming a thing of the past.[10]

In spite of all the arguments favoring the predominantly outside board, the tendency is to increase the number of insiders. There is, of course, no assurance that an outside board will give the affairs of the corporation the attention that they need. Outsiders can easily

[6] Gerard Swope, "Some Aspects of Corporate Management," *Harvard Business Review*, XXIII, No. 3 (Spring, 1945), 316.

[7] S. J. Weinberg, "A Corporation Director Looks at His Job," *Harvard Business Review*, XXIII, No. 3 (Spring, 1945), 316.

[8] *New York Times*, June 28, 1922, p. 23.

[9] Quoted in J. C. Baker, *Directors and Their Functions*, Boston: Harvard Graduate School of Business Administration, 1945, p. 5.

[10] Lewis D. Gilbert, "Management and the Public Stockholder," *Harvard Business Review*, XXVIII, No. 4 (July, 1950), 78.

become "yes men" for the chief executive, whether through friendship or inertia. They may even be selected in the first place by the chief executive to be essentially a dummy board.[11]

As in all organizational matters, mere machinery cannot assure results. Everything depends on the individuals holding the positions. It is generally agreed that the Standard Oil Company of New Jersey, which is an outstanding example of the inside board, has a very effective organization.[12] And the same is true of Bethlehem Steel Corporation.

Such light as this study sheds on this controversial issue consists of the following findings. In the first place, it shows that whatever the merits of the case, the proportion of officers on the boards, except for the railroads, is increasing.[13] In the second place, it indicates that the objection to inside boards often mentioned—that they will be overgenerous in the determination of their own salaries—is not supported by actual practice. Comparison of the financial compensation of presidents and board chairmen of industrial corporations with half or more of their boards made up of officers with the compensation of the presidents and board chairmen in corporations which have taken more than half of their board members from outside the company shows the median compensation to be higher for the latter group.[14]

A third finding, which is of interest in comparing the inside and outside boards, is that the proportion of officers is appreciably larger on the boards of fast-growing companies than on the boards of slow-growing or static companies, as shown in Table 7. Nearly two-thirds (64.3 percent) of the boards of the fast-growing companies had more officers than outsiders on the board, as compared with only one-third (33.3 percent) for the slow-growing companies as a whole, and only one in eight for the declining companies. The companies in-

[11] The fact that board members, outside and inside, are usually nominated by the chief executive is frequently noted. See, e.g., W. T. Blair, "Appraising the Board of Directors," *Harvard Business Review*, XXVIII, No. 1 (January, 1950), 102; Swope, "Some Aspects of Corporate Management," *Harvard Business Review*, XXIII, No. 3 (Spring, 1945), 315; and Gordon, *Business Leadership*, p. 121.

[12] All members of the board are full-time employees on salary, although several hold no other office than that of director of the company.

[13] See Table 5 above.

[14] See Table 62 below and discussion accompanying it, p. 128.

cluded in this analysis are all industrials whose assets multiplied at least five times between 1924 and 1949 at one extreme, and those whose assets did not double during this period at the other extreme. While the change in assets is not an infallible test of successful management, it seems probable that it is closely related to it. The number of bankers also is included in Table 7, since it appears to be of interest in this connection. All the comparisons in Table 7 show that the fast-growing companies have relatively more officers and fewer bankers than the slow-growing companies.

The question immediately presents itself as to whether differences in the composition of the board have contributed to the rate of growth or whether the rate of growth has influenced the composition of the board. As a check, the composition of the boards of eight companies whose assets decreased during this twenty-five year period was analyzed for 1924. These companies, being apparently the least successful, seemed to be the most likely candidates for changes in the board. They had fewer officers (39.5 percent) and more bankers (19.3 percent) on their boards than the slow-growing companies grouped with them. The composition of their boards in 1924 was found to be similar to that in 1949, except that they had even more bankers and fewer officers in the earlier year than in 1949. In short, no change appears to have been made in the composition of their boards because of their difficulties.

There are, of course, other related variables that might have more influence on the composition of the board than the rate of growth. Some of these appear to be the age of the company, its size, and its financial structure. Consequently, the composition of the boards of directors of a sample of the industrial companies, grouped according to these factors, has been analyzed and summarized in Table 7. This shows that differences related to age and size are too small to be significant. But it is important to remember that all the corporations included have assets in excess of $75,000,000. Other studies have shown marked differences for corporations of different sizes when the range included is greater.[15]

[15] See discussion on p. 35 below.

There are important differences, however, in the composition of the boards of the heavily indebted and of debt-free companies, the latter having fewer officers and more bankers than the former. This is true both for the fast-growing companies and for the slow-growing

TABLE 7

PERCENTAGE OF BOARD MEMBERSHIP CONSISTING OF COMPANY OFFICERS AND BANKERS IN SELECTED GROUPS OF INDUSTRIAL CORPORATIONS, 1952

	COMPANY OFFICERS			BANKERS		
CORPORATIONS	All	Fast Growing a	Slow Growing b	All	Fast Growing a	Slow Growing b
Older c	54.2	55.9	53.2	15.6	13.2	17.0
Younger d	54.1	58.7	45.5	15.3	13.5	18.8
Larger e	54.2	58.5	49.0	16.2	12.0	21.2
Smaller f	53.9	56.4	51.7	15.7	14.9	16.3
Heavily indebted g j	62.3	68.3	55.9	11.4	8.4	14.6
Debt free h j	53.7	55.0	51.8	14.3	13.2	15.8
All k	57.0	57.6	49.9	15.6	13.3	18.0

a Companies with assets in 1949 more than five times assets in 1924.
b Companies with assets in 1949 less than double assets in 1924.
c Companies operating before 1900.
d Companies organized 1900 or later.
e Companies with assets in excess of $160,000,000.
f Companies with assets of $160,000,000 or less.
g Companies with funded debts and bank loans equal to 25 percent or more of total assets.
h Companies with funded debts and bank loans equal to less than 5 percent of total assets.
j In order to include all the heavily indebted and debt-free companies in these groups, the fast-growing companies have been defined as those with assets in 1949 three times or more those in 1924, and the slow-growing companies include all with assets in 1949 less than three times those in 1924.
k Includes 42 fast-growing and 42 slow-growing companies for the corporations classified by age and size. For the heavily indebted and debt-free companies there are 39 fast-growing and 33 slow-growing companies.

ones. Equally striking is the difference between the boards of the fast-growing and slow-growing companies. In every grouping given, the fast-growing companies have more officers and fewer bankers than the slow-growing ones.

The importance of financial problems has usually dictated the presence of bankers on boards of directors. All the railroads and all but seven of the public utilities whose boards have been included in the sample in Table 8 have either commercial or investment bankers, and often both, on their boards. One-fourth of the industrials, on the other hand, have no bankers at all. This may be attributed to the greater degree of self-financing among the industrials than among

TABLE 8

COMPOSITION OF THE BOARD OF DIRECTORS IN 1952 [a]

| | TOTAL | RAILROAD | PUBLIC UTILITIES | INDUSTRIAL | | |
				Total	Smaller	Larger
Number of com- panies	170	27	49	94	47	47
Number of directors	2,309	392	609	1,308	587	721
Median assets in mil- lions of dollars	296	566	286	268	152	442
PRINCIPAL OCCUPATION BY PERCENTAGE DISTRIBUTION						
Active officers	41.0	16.1	28.9	54.1	51.6	56.0
Retired officers	2.2	.8	1.3	3.0	3.6	2.5
Commercial bankers	11.4	18.6	11.5	9.3	8.9	9.6
Investment bankers [b]	6.9	8.7	6.9	6.3	6.0	6.6
Insurance company officers	2.5	4.6	3.4	1.5	1.7	1.2
Individual investors	2.1	1.0	1.0	2.9	3.1	2.8
Other business	22.4	33.9	31.2	14.8	15.5	14.3
Lawyers	5.9	8.2	9.2	3.7	4.6	2.9
All other [c]	5.7	8.2	6.6	4.5	5.1	4.0
	100.0	100.0	100.0	100.0	100.0	100.0

[a] Data from individual company notices of annual meetings of stockholders. The largest companies were used for this tabulation, insofar as the notices give this information.

[b] Includes also a few brokers.

[c] Engineers, representatives of the general public (including one housewife), etc.

the other corporations. But it does not explain the greater number of bankers on the boards of the debt-free companies than on the boards of the heavily indebted industrials. A further breakdown of the data shows that the companies with large debts have a larger proportion of investment bankers—6.2 percent as compared with 5.2 percent. But in view both of the great diversity in the composition of boards of directors of the companies under review and the relatively small sample, this small differential may be due to chance.

Moreover, the larger number of commercial bankers on the boards of the debt-free companies brings the total number of bankers on the boards of these companies above that of the companies with large debts.

Table 8 gives the occupations of all directors for railroads and public utilities as well as industrials. The industrial companies in this sample were selected without reference to rate of growth or indebtedness. They include the larger companies as far as the data could be found. No company with assets under $75,000,000 was included. This table shows that the percentage of bankers on the railroad boards is greater than the percentage of their own officers. This is in sharp contrast to the proportions for the industrial boards. The railroads also have a large representation from other kinds of business, even larger than from the bankers, whereas the industrials have fewer representatives of other business than of bankers. The public utilities fall between the extremes presented by the railroads and industrials.

The industrial companies have chosen to weight their boards heavily with their own officers and have, in consequence, comparatively few places left for other businessmen. They also have few outside lawyers. The occupational distribution of outside directors found for the very large industrial corporations is quite different from that in small ones, as shown by a National Industrial Conference Board study.[16] This does not classify directors' occupations according to size of the company, but the majority of directors included are in smaller companies than those of this study. The National Industrial Conference Board group contains a much larger proportion of investors on the boards than has been found among the large companies of the present study. Also, the National Industrial Conference Board directors have a much larger representation of lawyers and relatively fewer bankers than the large industrials.

Investors as such have little representation in the large companies, even when insurance officials are grouped with the investors. Labor unions have no representation at all. There is a growing tendency,

[16] "The Corporate Directorship," in *Studies in Business Policy*, No. 63 (1953), p. 9.

however, to appoint representatives of the general public. These are usually distinguished professional men—quite frequently university presidents. The number of women is extremely small, although a scattered few who have inherited a substantial block of stock in the family corporation do hold directorships. Only one woman was found who was not a larger investor—a "housewife" on the board of a large power company. Mr. Young's recent action in including a woman on the board of the New York Central is almost unique. The nonbusiness representation is small, but it does indicate recognition of the "public" interest. Only one instance has been found of a corporation being required to include a representative of the general public on its board. This is the governor of Illinois, *ex officio,* on the board of the Illinois Central Railroad.

There is a good deal of evidence that chance and early precedent, as much as any demonstrated needs of the different enterprises, are responsible for variations in the membership of the boards of directors. The Standard Oil Company had a one-hundred-percent inside board fifty years ago, and several of the Standard Oil companies today have such boards. The original American Tobacco Company had a board made up primarily of officers, although supplemented by a few organizers and large investors. Today, the American Tobacco Company and several other tobacco companies have boards made up entirely of insiders. And whereas the United States Steel Corporation had very few officers on its board when it was first organized, and has only two today, its competitor, Bethlehem Steel, has always had a large number of officers on its board and has had no outside representation at all for many years.

The National Industrial Conference Board study states that many of the companies canvassed indicated a desire to achieve a balanced board, i.e., a board with representation from (1) the company management, (2) outside interests, (3) large investors, and (4) experts in general management. The last group includes executives in other comparable businesses and financial, legal, and other professional experts.[17]

Applying this test to the corporations of this study, 59.3 percent

[17] "The Corporate Directorship," in *Studies in Business Policy,* No. 63 (1953), p. 4.

of the railroad boards meet the test, but only 22.5 percent of the public utility and 27.7 percent of the industrial boards have representation from all four of these groups; and, of course, the 7.7 percent of the boards with wholly inside boards have only one of these groups represented. Forty percent of the boards lack representatives both of the large investors and the general public. This indicates that the well-balanced board is not really regarded as important. Otherwise a larger number of corporations would presumably have taken steps to achieve it.

INTERLOCKING DIRECTORATES

One further analysis of boards of directors has been made for this study. This is the extent of interlocking directorates for this particular group of companies. The sample selected was all railroads, public utilities, and industrial companies with assets in excess of $50,-000,000 in 1949 as listed in *Moody's Manuals*. This includes a few corporations in the 50-to-75-million group that have not been included in the analysis of chief executives. For 1900 it includes all corporations in *Moody's Manuals* with assets in excess of $16,000,000. The number of interlocking directorates is given in Table 9.

The proportion of directors that held no directorships in a large company besides their own is a little larger for 1949 than for 1900— 87 percent as compared with 83 percent. The most striking difference between the two periods, however, is in the upper end of the scale. Although the number of directors for the recent period is nearly three times that for the earlier period, there are more individuals holding more than five directorships for the 1900 directors. And the maximum number of directorships for the earlier period, sixteen, is just double that for the recent period.[18]

The decline in the number of interlocking directorates among the large corporations is partly the result of the legal limitations that have been placed on such interlocking since the earlier period, but partly also of the tendency to draw more and more on the inside group. That such interlocking directorates are still useful in reaching

---

[18] The 16 directorships in 1900 were held by R. M. Gallaway, banker. The 8 directorships in 1949 were held by Sidney J. Weinberg, investment banker. In neither case are their directorships in financial companies included.

agreements with competitors is illustrated by the instance, cited by Quinn, of General Electric calling on the services of one of its banking directors, who was also a director of General Motors, when the price competition in electric refrigerators became too severe.[19] However, a great many companies have no interlocking with other large

TABLE 9

NUMBER OF INTERLOCKING DIRECTORATES IN
LARGE CORPORATIONS, 1900 AND 1949 [a]

NUMBER OF DIRECTORATES	NUMBER OF DIRECTORS	
	1900	*1949*
1	1,442	4,256
2	187	441
3	39	110
4	32	46
5	14	10
6	9	4
7	5	2
8	1	1
9–16	5	. . .
	1,734	4,870

 [a] Compiled from *Moody's Manuals* of industrials, railroads, and public utilities. Does not include directorates in large financial companies. The boards included in this study are those of railroads, public utilities, and industrials with assets in excess of $16,000,000 in 1900 and $50,000,000 in 1949. These lower limits are roughly comparable in terms of purchasing power of the dollar as indicated by indexes of wholesale prices for the two years. Subsidiary companies are not included in this tabulation.

companies, and some—e.g., the Bethlehem Steel Corporation, do not permit their inside boards to hold any outside directorships.[20]

The number of directorships held by the chief executives included in this study is given in Table 10. The data were obtained from biographical sources as well as from the tabulation of directorships from *Moody's Manuals* and are not limited to the larger corporations. Also, they include directorships in subsidiaries and in financial companies. The data are necessarily incomplete, but the comparisons for the different periods and for the different sizes of corporations and kinds of business should be fairly dependable.

[19] T. K. Quinn, *Giant Business*, New York: Exposition Press, 1953, p. 97.
[20] "Bethlehem Steel," *Fortune*, XXXIII, No. 4 (April, 1941), 140.

TABLE 10

OUTSIDE DIRECTORSHIPS HELD BY PRESIDENTS AND
CHAIRMEN OF LARGE CORPORATIONS

OUTSIDE DIRECTORSHIPS	NUMBER OF OFFICERS			PERCENTAGE OF OFFICERS		
	1900	1925	1950	1900	1925	1950
None	139	104	237	44.0	31.5	26.9
1–9	133	166	548	42.0	50.3	62.2
10 or more	44	60	97	14.0	18.2	10.9
	316	330	882	100.0	100.0	100.0

This analysis of the number of outside directorships held by top officials of large corporations shows an increase in the number of directorships held in the first quarter of this century, and a decrease in the second quarter. The breakdown for 1950, given in Table 11, shows the largest proportion of those holding 10 or more directorships to be railroad officials, and the smallest proportion the indus-

TABLE 11

OUTSIDE DIRECTORSHIPS OF PRESIDENTS AND BOARD CHAIRMEN IN
DIFFERENT SIZES OF CORPORATIONS AND DIFFERENT
KINDS OF BUSINESS, 1950

OUTSIDE DIRECTORSHIPS	ASSETS IN MILLIONS OF DOLLARS				KIND OF BUSINESS		
	Under 100	100– 249	250– 499	500 and over	Railroad	Public Utility	Industrial
None	28.7	32.7	23.7	17.3	18.3	26.4	28.3
1–9	64.4	59.5	62.1	62.6	50.5	64.3	63.3
10 or more	6.9	7.7	14.2	20.1	31.2	9.3	8.4
	100.0	100.0	100.0	100.0	100.0	100.0	100.0

trial corporation officials. Thus the industrial corporations not only tend to rely heavily on their own officers for their boards of directors, foregoing the contacts that outside directors would provide, but they have fewer contacts than the railroads and public utilities through directorships held by their own chief executives in other companies. The table also shows a larger proportion of the officers of the very large corporations holding outside directorships than those of the small corporations. The principal reason for this is that a very large number of these multiple directorships are directorships in subsidiary corporations, which have been included but which are not strictly outside directorships. Nevertheless, there are still a good many executives of large corporations—although relatively fewer than in earlier years—who hold directorships in a number of large and unrelated corporations.

SUMMARY

The most important conclusion to be drawn from this study of boards of directors is that the large corporations, and more particularly the industrial corporations, are depending increasingly on inside boards. But while this appears to deprive them of the perspective and fresh approach of an outside group and might result in favoring one's immediate associates, whether they merit it or not, at the possible expense of the stockholders, the actual records of corporations with inside boards tend to be better than those of the corporations with outside boards.

Between the typical inside board of today and that of the earlier period there are two important differences which may account for the apparent current success of this type of board. Today it is rarely made up of officers appointed and dominated by a small group of stockholders and bankers. The subordinate officers are usually the appointees of the president, but his authority is not likely to be exercised with the same degree of arbitrariness as that of the owner-president, and the chance of decisions being reached after consideration by a group of officers appears to be better than in the board dominated by the owner-president or by bankers and stockholders interested in a quick profit. The other factor, related to this, is the professionalization of business leadership. The officers for the most part have had longer experience with the company and are more likely to identify their interests with those of the company. They tend to have a professional pride in its success.

These factors may account for the apparent superiority of the inside board. But to the extent that it prevails, the accepted system of checks and balances, which the relationship of the board to the stockholders on the one hand and the officers on the other was designed to provide, is disappearing.

CHAPTER FOUR

ORIGINS
OF BUSINESS LEADERS:
NATIONALITY, RELIGION
AND POLITICS

I congratulate poor young men upon being born to that ancient and honourable degree which renders it necessary that they should devote themselves to hard work. A basketful of bonds is the heaviest basket a young man ever had to carry.

ANDREW CARNEGIE

The best time during the history of the United States for the poor boy ambitious for high business success to have been born was around the year 1835. Since then the proportion of those in his position who realized their hopes has definitely declined, despite the steady growth in the total numbers of the elite.

C. WRIGHT MILLS

THERE has been a lively interest lately among scholars in the social sciences concerning the origins of business leaders. And Carnegie's contention that poverty is an asset rather than a liability has been sharply challenged. If the chances of the underprivileged reaching the top are declining, or were always very slight, as some insist, this is a matter of real concern. No merit system can be expected to work perfectly. But if wealth and social status are all but indispensable conditions of success, the group from which top talent is chosen is restricted indeed.

It is recognized that formal education and a record of ability are

The quotations at the head of this chapter are taken from Andrew Carnegie, *The Empire of Business*, New York: Doubleday, 1916, p. 19, and C. Wright Mills, "The American Business Elite," *Journal of Economic History*, Supplement V (1945), p. 44.

not the only factors in getting started on the road to success. Social acceptability, by whatever standards this may be judged, knowing the "right" people, and sometimes financial backing are important. All these things are greatly influenced by the family background. Consequently, some of the more tangible factors in the family background of the chief executives have been included in this study.

FOREIGN-BORN

Insofar as there is discrimination in employment or business dealings on account of sex, race, nationality, religion, and politics, it will probably be most apparent at the top levels. And it may be said without further comment that no woman and no Negro has been found among the top executives of this study. There are, however, a few foreign-born. These are listed in Table 12. The proportion of foreign-born among the executives is lower than the proportion in the total United States population, but in view of the many handicaps of this group it is surprising to find it as high as it is.

Further analysis of the origins of the foreign-born executives, however, shows that the majority are English speaking. In fact, the proportion of Canadians in the 1950 group far exceeds the proportion of Canadian-born in the total population.[1] All of the foreign-born of the 1900 group were either Canadian or West European. One East European is found in the 1925 group, and in the 1950 group there are nine East or South Europeans and three who are neither European nor Canadian. These three are Wilfred Sykes of Inland Steel, from New Zealand; Sosthenes Behn of International Telephone and Telegraph (appearing both in the 1925 and 1950 groups), born in the Virgin Islands of "Danish and French extraction"; and the Bolivian, Antenor Patino. The last is not a resident of the United States, and his company's properties are in Bolivia. The company was established by his father and only later was incorporated in Delaware with a number of American officers. Thus it is clear that no wholly American corporation in the group under consideration is directed by an officer who is not either American by birth or of European descent.

[1] No French Canadians are found among the executives.

No thoroughgoing study of the origins of second-generation Americans has been attempted, but the names suggest European, and for the most part North and West European, ancestry. The only exception that has been noted is James B. Haggin, of the 1900 executive group, who had a Turkish grandfather.

TABLE 12

FOREIGN-BORN EXECUTIVES [a]

NUMBER OF FOREIGN-BORN

Country of Birth	1900	1925	1950
Canada	5	3	17
Great Britain	7	9	11
Ireland	7	4	3
Germany	5	2	1
Scandinavia	. .	. .	6
Other European	1	2	11
All other	. .	1	3
Total	25	21	52

PERCENTAGE OF FOREIGN-BORN

	1900	1925	1950
In total U.S. population [b]	13.3	13.6	11.5
Among executives	8.8	6.6	6.0

PERCENTAGE OF ENGLISH-SPEAKING [c]

	1900	1925	1950
In U.S. foreign-born population	52.3	32.8	22.1
Among foreign-born executives	76.0	76.2	61.5

[a] Excluding the sons of American citizens born abroad.

[b] 1880, 1905, and 1930 have been used for this comparison, since the average age of the foreign-born population is much lower than that of the executives. The 1905 foreign-born were assumed to be the average of the 1900 and 1910 numbers.

[c] Those born in Great Britain, Ireland, Canada, Australia, and New Zealand.

Even among the Europeans, the proportion reaching the top bears little relation to the proportion in the country. It has already been noted that the English speaking have disproportionate representation among the foreign-born in each group. And the South and East Europeans are correspondingly underrepresented. The small number of these who are found among the 1950 executives are mostly in the merchandising and entertainment fields. And with only two exceptions, Sosthenes Behn and Philip Sporn, the foreign-born public utility and railroad executives are English, Irish, and Canadian.

Many of the foreign-born who reached the top were, like Andrew

Carnegie, brought to this country by their parents as children and had the advantages and handicaps of second-generation Americans rather than those of the foreign-born. And a number who came without their parents, as adults, had independent means. Among these were Henry Fink, of the Norfolk and Western Railroad, and August Heckscher, president of various corporations. Others came as representatives of successful foreign enterprises.

The chances of an immigrant with the triple handicap of foreign birth, poverty, and no American schooling reaching the top were slight.[2] Some have been found, however, who did succeed without financial assistance and without any education in American schools. Marcus Daly of Amalgamated Copper "came to New York a young boy without money or acquaintances, got a job as errand boy in a store," and eventually worked up to the top.[3] Franz A. Assmann of American Can came from Germany alone, without knowing English and without money, and obtained a job as apprentice in a New York City tin shop through an employment agency, although he had no previous training in the work.[4] And Fritz Sitterding of Virginia Passenger and Power "came to this country as an immigrant at 18 'with a saw and hammer under his arm'" and "worked as a carpenter at $1.00 a day."[5]

Among the 1925 executives, Robert E. M. Cowie of American Railway Express "travelled to the United States by steerage" when he was about seventeen and "became an office boy . . . at $30 a month."[6] And Adolf Zukor, coming to America at fifteen, "had with him twenty-five dollars sewed in the lining of his clothing." He started as "a sweeper in a furrier's shop, earning two dollars a week."[7] Zukor is included in both the 1925 and 1950 groups. Finally, Spyros

---

[2] One might agree with Carnegie that these are not really handicaps; that habits of industry and thrift and the drive to escape poverty are more important than a good education and social position. But the data of this study do not lend much support to such a position.

[3] *Harpers Weekly*, Nov. 24, 1900, p. 1117.

[4] According to a letter from his son, Frank A. Assmann, Dec. 4, 1953: "There is a belief in the family that when he arrived here he had only four Marks, then about 96 cents, in his pocket."

[5] Letter from a former business associate of Mr. Sitterding.

[6] *New York Times*, June 23, 1934, p. 13.

[7] *Current Biography*, 1950, p. 640.

Skouras, of the 1950 executives, came to the United States at seven-teen. A brother who had come before him assisted him to get here, as he himself assisted other brothers later, but he had no schooling in the United States and earned his way from the beginning, start-ing as a busboy.[8]

While these six exhaust the list of documented cases that have been found, there have been a number of executives who were brought to the United States by their parents and received some schooling here but who received no further assistance from their families. And there were also a few, mostly Canadians, who made their own way, but who started their careers in other countries be-fore coming to the United States. The proportion of men from poor families is much higher among the foreign-born executives, whether or not the parents themselves came to this country, than among the American-born executives. Twelve out of 25 foreign-born execu-tives in the 1900 group came from poor families; 6 out of 21 in the 1925 group; and 10 out of 52 in the 1950 group.[9] This is probably to be explained by the fact that immigration is a selective process and that, in consequence, the foreign-born group had more than the usual number of able and ambitious men who could overcome unusual difficulties. William Miller is correct in maintaining that the typical business leader early in this century was *not* an immigrant, but he appears to underestimate the degree of poverty among those who were immigrants when he states that "scarcely two or three [of his eighteen foreign-born business leaders] fit the historians' concept of the *poor* immigrant who made good, and even these men had been brought to the United States at . . . an early age.[10]

[8] *Current Biography,* 1943, p. 702.

[9] The percentages from poor families for all executives are 12, 16, and 12 percent respectively.

[10] William Miller, "American Historians and the Business Elite," *Journal of Economic History,* IX, No. 2 (November, 1949), 200–201. This is partly to be explained by differences in the list of executives, but four of the eight foreign-born who are included in both studies (Assmann, Brady, Callaway, and Chisholm) are classified as poor here, and one of them, Assmann, came to the United States as an adult. Callaway went to work at thirteen after his father (a merchant) had lost his property and died. Chisholm also made his own way from thirteen on, following his father's death. And Brady became a store clerk at thirteen.

RELIGIOUS AFFILIATIONS

Church membership is another factor in the family background that may play a role in business success. The prestige that derives from the British tradition extends to membership in the Episcopalian and—to a somewhat lesser degree—the Presbyterian denominations. For the most part, the religious preference is inherited from the family, and the dominance of British family backgrounds is sufficient, in itself, to account for the large proportion of executives belonging to these churches. Geographic origins within the country are also influential in determining the number from the different denominations. There are many Congregationalists from New England, and Presbyterians, Methodists, and Baptists from the Southern states.

The data obtained on religious affiliations are incomplete. This is partly because this item was not included among those requested when letters asking for information were sent to the executives or members of their families. But there is a good deal of evidence that a large proportion of the executives do not belong to any church and have no strong denominational preference. The data found in published biographies are given in Table 13, and for 1950 a comparison has been made with the total membership of each religious body for the United States as a whole (see Table 14). It is clear that the Episcopalian membership among the executives is farthest out of line with its membership in the population as a whole, being more than ten times as high in the executive group as it is in the whole population. Presbyterian and Congregational memberships are also relatively high in the executive group. At the other extreme, the Roman Catholic group is relatively low. The difference in the proportions for the two Jewish groups is not large, but further analysis of the executive data reveals the fact that the Jewish members are heavily concentrated in the merchandising, entertainment, and mass communications fields. Very few are found in heavy industry or public utilities, and none at all among the railroad executives.

Catholics, on the other hand, have risen to the top in the railroad and public utility fields, and particularly in the latter, in greater proportions than in industry. The reason for this appears to be that

there are fewer executives from wealthy families in these fields, as
there are fewer wealthy families among the Catholic executives than
among the Protestant executives. In other words, there are fewer
inheritors and investors, and more who have worked their way to
the top, in the public utility and railroad corporations than in the in-

TABLE 13

RELIGIOUS PREFERENCES OF EXECUTIVES

	NUMBER OF EXECUTIVES			TOTAL MEMBERSHIP IN U.S.A., 1950 [a]
RELIGIOUS PREFERENCE	1900	1925	1950	(in millions)
Episcopalian	67	70	118	2.5
Presbyterian	30	53	89	3.1
Methodist	21	17	39	8.9
Roman Catholic	13	22	35	28.6
Congregational	14	10	27	1.2
Baptist	3	11	22	16.5
Jewish	6	9	18	5.0
Lutheran	1	. . .	10	5.9
Unitarian	6	7	8	0.1
All other	15	10	24	15.0
Total	176	209	390	86.8
No preference given	140	121	492	63.9 [b]

[a] *Statistical Abstract of the United States.*
[b] This includes children too young for church membership.

dustrial corporations; and since the Catholics are found in larger
proportions among those that worked their way, they are likewise
found in larger proportions in the kinds of business where executives
who have worked their way up are found with greatest frequency.[11]
This does not explain the absence of Jews among railroad officials,
since the Jewish executives, like the Catholic, come in disproportionate numbers from poor families.

[11] The smaller proportion of railway executives from wealthy families is at least
partly explained by the fact that the railroad corporations were older than the others
and there had been a gradual dispersion of control. The high proportion of Roman
Catholics may also be accounted for in part by the fact that they are the sons and
grandsons of Irish immigrants who went into railroad construction at the bottom in
large numbers in the era of railroad development. Specific instances have been found
to support this view, but no quantitative data are available. The Roman Catholics
among the public utility executives may possibly be accounted for by the earlier ties
between many of these companies and local political machines, together with the
fact that the Irish tended to be active in politics. Most of the Catholic officials appear
to be Irish in origin, but no actual cases of a direct political heritage have been found.

There are marked differences between the Jewish and Catholic groups in the way in which they reached the top. Forty percent of the Jewish group organized their own enterprises, as compared with only 7 percent of the Catholic group. And none of the Jews was selected for success in another company, whereas 19 percent of the Catholics were. The proportion that worked up within the corporation is large in each group, although a little below the average for the Jews. The total number of cases is small, however, and consequently these proportions are not completely reliable.

TABLE 14

PERCENTAGE DISTRIBUTION OF MEMBERSHIP IN RELIGIOUS BODIES

Religious Body	1950 Executives	Total U.S. Population
Episcopalian	30.3	2.9
Presbyterian	22.8	3.6
Methodist	10.0	10.2
Roman Catholic	8.9	32.9
Congregational	6.9	1.4
Baptist	5.7	19.0
Jewish	4.6	5.8
Lutheran	2.6	6.8
Unitarian	2.1	0.1
All other	6.2	17.3
	100.0	100.0

In most instances the religious preference reflects the family background from which the individuals come, but there is some evidence that church membership is occasionally changed to conform with the group with which they eventually associate. Five cases have been found in which the sons of clergymen have changed their religions from those of their fathers, and in each case upward in the social scale.[12] That is, a Methodist may shift to the Presbyterian faith, and a Presbyterian to Episcopalian, but not vice versa. One case was found of a Catholic executive whose son (also an executive) was Episcopalian. Whether such changes are a natural adaptation to environment or a deliberate move to improve social and economic status

[12] The test of social scale used here is that found in the Federal Council of the Churches of Christ in America, *Information Service*, XXVII (May 15, 1946), 3. This shows, for the religious groups cited here, that the percentage of upper-class members is 24 for Episcopalians, 22 for Presbyterians, 13 for Methodists, and 9 for Catholics.

has not been learned, and the data are fragmentary at best, since no thorough study has been made of this aspect of family backgrounds.

POLITICAL AFFILIATIONS

Political affiliations, like religious affiliations, have been noted as far as they are available in published biographies, but no effort has been made to increase the list by correspondence with individual executives or their families. The larger proportion for which information is available, as compared with religious affiliations, is partly due to the fact that the individuals concerned are more likely to have a political preference than a religious preference. It is difficult to imagine a top corporation official who is politically indifferent.[13]

TABLE 15

POLITICAL AFFILIATION OF EXECUTIVES
(Percentage distribution)

	1900	1925	1950
Republican	72.9	78.1	75.9
Democrat	25.6	19.0	20.3
Both	1.5	2.1	. . .
Independent	. . .	0.8	3.8
	100.0	100.0	100.0
Number of cases included	199	242	476
Political party not given	117	88	406

The great preponderance of Republicans in this group, as shown in Table 15, is to be expected. There are no marked trends over the period covered, and very little difference between small and large corporation officials. There is, however, an appreciable difference between the industrial, public utility, and railroad officials, as shown in Table 16. Whether this is due to the differences in geographical origins of the different groups or to differences in their political interests is not clear. One official was found who changed his party be-

[13] The larger proportion of cases found in 1925, as compared with 1900 and 1950, is partly due to the fact that biographical data are more complete for this group than for the others, and partly to the fact that, through the courtesy of Louise Overacker, the writer had access to unpublished records compiled for a study of money in elections that covered a period closely corresponding to that during which the 1925 group was most active.

cause of his growing interest in the protective tariff, but for the most part no mention of political interests was found in the biographical data, beyond the record of the party.

TABLE 16

PERCENTAGE OF REPUBLICANS AMONG EXECUTIVES OF DIFFERENT TYPES OF BUSINESS [a]

	1900	1925	1950
Railroads	63.6	68.2	69.8
Public utilities	76.3	79.5	71.4
Industrials	77.9	80.5	77.2
Largest companies [b]	71.1	75.8	75.9
Smallest companies [b]	72.6	76.4	78.9

[a] Among those executives whose political affiliations were found.
[b] See p. 14 for classification of companies by amount of assets.

Although many executives have held government positions at some time in their career, few have combined an active political career with business.[14] An important exception is found to this, however, among the public utility executives of the early period. To illustrate, D. B. Hasbrouck went from a position as clerk of the Metropolitan Police Commission of New York to various offices with the City's ferry and street railway companies and ultimately became president of the Metropolitan Street Railway. James Jourdan was president of the Brooklyn Police Department before he became president of the Brooklyn Union Gas Company. Albert Carlton became president of the United Electric Company of New Jersey while he continued to hold office as Comptroller of Elizabeth. And Andrew Hickenlooper served as lieutenant-governor of Ohio during his presidency of the Cincinnati Gas and Electric Company.

This kind of association was more acceptable then than now. Such political activities as the present day executives engage in are more likely to be in the interest of the business they represent than for their own personal interest. And this type of activity is not apt to

[14] At least one in four has held some government position, mostly part time and unpaid, the greatest number being advisory positions related to their business experience. A good many, however, have held full-time professional positions at some time in their careers. Military service in war time has not been included in the record of government service.

result in holding public office. The 1950 executive group of this study lost four members to the Eisenhower administration, two of them to cabinet positions. But they not only resigned from their business positions; they disposed of their stock. And the ensuing publicity concerning their stockholdings in the corporations they headed made it very clear that the separation of business and political activities is taken seriously by the general public.

This does not mean, of course, that the separation of business and government is complete. A great many junior officers in the corporations—and occasionally high executives—have been lured from government positions, not because they had exceptional ability but because they had specialized information, or influence in government circles, that might be useful to the business hiring them. And there are many connections between business and government that are not obvious to the layman. But the chief executive is not likely to be active in both fields at once; nor is he likely to get his job in the first place, as some of the early public utility executives did, as a result of political pressures.

CHAPTER FIVE

ORIGINS
OF BUSINESS LEADERS:
FATHERS' OCCUPATIONS
AND INCOME

To the extent that business leaders of the present generation are drawn from the "big business" class, inbreeding may be said to characterize the group responsible for the control and direction of American business. . . . There is reason to believe that the representation of this class among business leaders is tending to increase as time goes on.

F. W. TAUSSIG AND C. S. JOSLYN

ONE of the factors in the family background which contributes most to the success of the future executive is likely to be his father's occupation. This usually determines, or is related to, the family income and the family's social position. Moreover, even when the son does not inherit a family business he still may be influenced by his father to follow in his footsteps, particularly if his father has been successful.

FATHERS' OCCUPATIONS

The occupations of the fathers of the executives of this study are recorded in Table 17. This Table shows a number of marked shifts in the importance of the different occupational groups in the three different periods. Some of these reflect changes in the total occupational distribution of the male population of the United States. To illustrate, the farmers among the fathers of executives declined from 21 percent in 1900 to 13 percent in 1950. This compares with a de-

The quotation at the head of this chapter is taken from Taussig and Joslyn, *American Business Leaders,* New York: Macmillan, 1932, p. 97.

cline in farmers in the total male population between 1870 and 1910 from 28 to 20 percent. Also, the proportion of workers, skilled and unskilled, has increased in both groups, although it remains very small among the fathers of executives as compared with the male population as a whole. Independent businessmen, on the other hand, have declined, relatively, in the whole population but have held their own among the business executives' fathers, the percentage being 48.7 for the 1900 executives and 48.4 for the 1950 executives.[1] And whereas the proportion of professional men increased for the entire male population from 2.3 percent in 1870 to 3.1 percent in 1910, it declined for the fathers of business executives from 22.4 percent for the 1900 group to 17.8 for the 1950 group.

TABLE 17

OCCUPATIONS OF THE FATHERS OF CORPORATION OFFICIALS [a]

OCCUPATION	NUMBER OF EXECUTIVES			PERCENTAGE DISTRIBUTION		
	1900	1925	1950	1900	1925	1950
Head of same corporation as son [b]	24	43	100	7.8	13.4	11.6
Independent business [c]						
Finance	17	21	48	5.5	6.7	5.5
Manufacture, mining, and transportation	52	33	77	16.9	10.2	8.9
Mercantile	44	41	136	14.2	12.8	15.8
Farming	64	48	115	20.8	15.0	13.4
Craft	9	11	29	2.9	3.4	3.4
Other	4	3	28	1.4	0.9	3.3
Total independent	190	157	433	61.7	49.0	50.2
Employee						
Official [d]	8	13	63	2.6	4.1	7.3
Sales	2	2	16	0.7	0.6	1.9
Clerical and minor administrative	2	11	32	0.7	3.4	3.7
Skilled labor	9	10	46	2.9	3.1	5.4
Semi-skilled and unskilled labor	4	10	18	1.3	3.1	2.1
Total employee	25	46	175	8.1	14.4	20.4

[1] This group comprises all those included in the independent business group in Table 17 except the farmers, and also the fathers who preceded their sons in the same corporation.

TABLE 17 *(continued)*

OCCUPATIONS OF THE FATHERS OF CORPORATION OFFICIALS

	NUMBER OF EXECUTIVES			PERCENTAGE DISTRIBUTION		
OCCUPATION	1900	1925	1950	1900	1925	1950
Professional						
Lawyer	16	21	44	5.2	6.6	5.1
M.D.	15	7	23	4.9	2.2	2.7
Clergyman	19	18	19	6.2	5.6	2.2
Teaching	6	9	20	1.9	2.8	2.3
Engineer	2	7	12	0.7	2.2	1.4
Public official e	5	8	11	1.6	2.5	1.3
Other	6	4	24	1.9	1.2	2.8
Total professional	69	74	153	22.4	23.1	17.8
Total	308	320	861	100.0	100.0	100.0
· No information	8	10	21			

a In some instances more than one occupation was found. In these cases the occupation in which the father was engaged at the time that the son was launched on his business career was used; if the timing of the different occupations was not available, the one indicated as the principal occupation was used.

b In some instances the business was not incorporated when the father headed it, so that this group includes both independent entrepreneurs and corporation officials. The number of these is smaller than the cases of inheritance owing to the fact that inheritance from other members of the family is not included here unless the other relative was also responsible for the individual's upbringing.

c In addition to individual entrepreneurs this includes corporation presidents who were the founders of the business. It does not include corporation officials who did not start the business or founders whose sons succeeded them.

d This includes only the upper ranks of corporation officials such as presidents, vice presidents, general managers, and treasurers.

e Mostly army officers.

Table 18 compares the percentage distribution of occupied males in the United States in 1910, with the percentage distribution of the occupations of fathers of business executives of the 1950 period. The proportion of business executives among the fathers of the executives is approximately seven times the proportion among the male population at large, and the proportion of professional men is nearly six times as large. At the other extreme the proportion of semiskilled and unskilled workers among the fathers of the executives is less than one-twentieth that for the entire male population. There are also relatively fewer farmers, clerical workers, and skilled workers among the fathers than among the total employed male population. The fact that the fathers, on the average, were somewhat older in

1910 than the employed population as a whole may have exaggerated these contrasts, but the differences cannot be explained primarily by this factor.

TABLE 18

COMPARISON OF OCCUPATIONS OF FATHERS OF 1950 EXECUTIVES
WITH OCCUPATIONS OF ENTIRE MALE POPULATION OF THE
UNITED STATES, 1910

OCCUPATION	PERCENTAGE DISTRIBUTION		RATIO OF FATHERS TO ENTIRE MALE POPULATION
	Employed Males, 1910 [a]	Fathers of 1950 Executives	
Semiskilled and un-skilled workers	45.4	2.1	.05:1
Farmers	19.9	13.4	.67:1
Skilled workers	14.5	5.4	.37:1
Clerical workers	9.2	5.6 [b]	.61:1
Business executives	7.9	55.7 [c]	6.96:1
Professionals	3.1	17.8	5.74.1

[a] Bureau of the Census, 16th Census, *Comparative Occupational Statistics, 1870–1940.*

[b] Includes clerical, minor administrative, and sales groups of Table 17.

[c] Includes corporation officials (both chief executives of same corporation as son and high officials of other corporations) and all independent businessmen except farmers.

It is, of course, to be expected that the business group, and particularly the top business group, will be disproportinately large among the fathers, since the sons themselves belong exclusively to this group. It is, rather, a tribute to the degree of occupational mobility in this country that only about one-third of the total group of business executives belong to the same general categories as their fathers. In each of the three periods covered, one-third of the fathers belonged to the group of corporation executives, or independent businessmen in the fields of finance, manufacture, mining, transportation, and public utilities.[2] And even within this group, a large proportion was in a business far removed from that of their fathers. If lawyers and engineers are added to the purely business group, something like two-fifths of all the fathers were in the same general

[2] 32.8 percent in 1900, 34.4 in 1925, and 33.3 in 1950. The mercantile group has not been included in this comparison since these are mostly small businessmen. Very few of the corporations included in this study are engaged in trade.

category of occupations as their sons. The comparison of the three periods shows no important changes in these proportions, although there is a slight rise in the percentages between the 1900 and 1925 group, and a slight decline between 1925 and 1950. When the occupations of the fathers of the more recent appointees of the 1950 executive group are compared with those for the older group, however, the decline in the proportion whose fathers were executives in related businesses is quite striking—28.2 percent for the younger and 39.9 percent for the older group (see Table 19).

The conclusion is reached in the Taussig and Joslyn study that the proportion of business leaders who are the sons of similar business leaders is increasing.[3] The 1925 data in the current study, which represent much the same generation as the business leaders of the Taussig and Joslyn study, appear to support this conclusion, although the increase over the 1900 group is very small. However, the 1950 group shows a slight decline from the 1925 group in these categories, and the decline for the younger 1950 executives is very marked. It appears in every subdivision of this general category, as shown in Table 19, although not among the lawyers and engineers.

Table 19 also shows a substantial increase in the younger group, as compared with the older, among those whose fathers were minor employees, whether white-collar or manual labor. In short, these data give no support whatever to the belief, frequently expressed, that inheritance is increasingly important.

Moreover, when a comparison is made of the occupations of the fathers of the 1950 executives, classified according to the size of the corporations of which the sons are chief executives, it appears that the larger corporations have a lower proportion of executives with fathers in the same category of business than the smaller corporations. These percentages are 36.7 for the smallest corporations, declining to 36.5, 31.8, and 23.4 respectively as the size class of the corporations rises. Also, the proportion of minor employees among the fathers is appreciably higher for the largest corporations than for the smallest, 18 percent as compared with 11 percent. This com-

[3] F. W. Taussig and C. S. Joslyn, *American Business Leaders*, New York, Macmillan, 1932, p. 97.

parison also is given in Table 19. The increase in the proportion of the "non-élite" among the current executives is confirmed by Keller's recent study comparing businessmen of 1870, 1900, and 1950.[4] Her percentages of fathers in the employee group do not differ materially from the ones in this study for 1900 and 1950. It is interesting to note, however, that her 1870 group showed a higher proportion of employee fathers than the 1900 group, although not so high as the 1950 group.

TABLE 19

COMPARISON OF SELECTED OCCUPATIONS OF FATHERS FOR OLDER AND YOUNGER EXECUTIVES AND EXECUTIVES IN THE SMALLEST AND LARGEST CORPORATIONS, 1950

(Percentage distribution)

Occupation	Older [a]	Younger [b]	Smallest Companies	Largest Companies
Head of same corporation as son	15.3	8.8	13.0	5.1
Executive in related business [c]	18.0	14.8	18.9	11.7
Finance executive	6.6	4.6	4.8	6.6
Lawyers	5.0	5.2	6.3	5.1
Engineers	.5	2.1	1.5	2.2
Employees [d]	10.2	15.2	11.2	18.4

[a] Those appointed prior to 1944.
[b] Those appointed 1944 or later.
[c] Includes corporation officials and independent owners of business in manufacture, mining, transportation, and public utilities.
[d] The groups included in Table 17 under sales, clerical and minor administrative, skilled, semi-skilled, and unskilled labor.

As has been noted earlier, the proportion of professional men was higher among the fathers of the 1900 executives than among those of 1950. Moreover, the largest number of professional men in the early group was the clergy, 19 in all, as compared with 16 lawyers and 15 of the medical profession. The explanation appears to lie partly in the high social esteem of the professions, giving these men contacts with the top business leaders, and partly in the fact that

[4] S. I. Keller, "The Social Origins and Career Lines of American Business Leaders," New York: Columbia University, 1953 (Ph.D. thesis, unpublished).

these men gave their sons a better education than the other men in the same income groups. A comparison of the 1900 and 1950 fathers' occupations shows that within the professions the clergy and medical professions have lost ground, the lawyers have held their own, and the engineers have increased, together with the miscellaneous professions.[5] The proportion of fathers in the professions has declined, but it is still large as compared with the population as a whole, and the younger 1950 group shows an increase over the older group in the number of sons of professional men—19.7 percent as compared with the 15.3 percent. These proportions are large for the reasons noted above and also because of the growing use of professional men in business. This last factor is particularly important in the younger 1950 group, accounting for most of the increase in the proportion of professional fathers as compared with the older group.

The proportion of fathers with an independent mercantile business is the largest group of all in 1950. These bear no direct relation to the sons' positions, since the number of mercantile corporations included in this study is extremely small. They are, rather, the representatives of small independent competitive businesses—the prototype of the entrepreneur of the free economy. At one end of the scale, they outnumber the fathers who preceded their sons in the same corporations; at the other end, they outnumber the employees (excluding high officials from this group); and they come close to equaling all the professional fathers combined. They outnumber other groups for every size of corporation and also among both the earlier and later appointees for this period. This group, of course, is an important one in the total population, but it was outnumbered by farmers in 1910, 5 to 1. Farmers have not contributed their proportionate share of sons to the business executives in any of these periods, although the farmers' sons outnumbered the tradesmen's sons in the 1900 group. Farmers, like merchants, are usually thought of as a model for the entrepreneurs of the free enterprise economy. The deficit of farmers' sons appears to be explained largely by the

[5] This last is partly because of an increase in the total number of callings in this group, but more specifically because of the increase of accountants and of other professions closely allied to business activities.

TABLE 20

COMPARISON OF OCCUPATIONS OF FATHERS FOR DIFFERENT
TYPES OF BUSINESS

(Percentage distribution)

Occupation		Railroad	Public Utility	Industrial
1900				
Head of same corporation as son		7.6	3.5	9.6
Independent businessmen		55.2	63.2	65.8
Merchants	14.3		19.3	12.3
Farmers	24.8		12.3	21.2
Other business	16.2		31.6	32.3
Employees		12.4	5.3	6.2
Corporation officials	4.8		. . .	2.1
Minor employees	7.6		5.3	4.1
Professional men		24.8	28.1	18.5
		100.0	100.0	100.0
1925				
Head of same corporation as son		3.0	7.7	18.3
Independent businessmen		37.9	53.8	51.5
Merchant	7.6		13.5	14.4
Farmer	16.7		15.4	14.4
Other business	13.6		24.9	22.7
Employees		24.2	11.5	11.9
Corporation officials	6.0		1.9	4.0
Minor employees	18.2		9.6	7.9
Professional men		34.9	26.9	18.3
		100.0	100.0	100.0
1950				
Head of same corporation as son		3.3	3.4	15.4
Independent businessmen		46.2	57.1	48.7
Merchant	12.1		14.1	16.9
Farmer	13.2		22.6	10.6
Other business	20.9		20.4	21.2
Employees		29.7	19.8	19.1
Corporation officials	7.7		5.6	7.7
Minor employees	22.0		14.2	11.4
Professional men		20.9	19.8	16.7
		100.0	100.0	100.0

geographic factor. It is less apparent among the railroad executives
than the public utility and industrial executives. The latter businesses,
being concentrated largely in the big cities, have not been within
as easy reach of the average farmer's son as the railroads running

through almost every small town. And so the farmer's son was more likely to become a messenger or telegraph operator for a railroad than the office boy of some public utility or industrial. The merchants' sons, on the contrary, were more likely to be within easy reach of the large public utilities and industrial concerns.

The most striking difference among the different types of enterprise, as shown by Table 20, is the comparatively high proportion of inherited positions among the industrials in each of the three periods. This is partly a reflection of the age of the different corporations. Most of the railroads were old enough in 1900 to make inheritance possible and too old for it to persist in the later periods. The industrials and the public utility corporations do not differ greatly in age distribution. They, too, were old enough for inheritance to diminish by 1950. But the average size of the industrials was smaller than that of the public utilities, and this also is a factor in inheritance. The proportion of employees is highest among the fathers of railroad executives in each of the periods recorded, for the same reason that inheritance is low.

TABLE 21

ENTREPRENEURIAL EXPERIENCE OF EXECUTIVES
AND OF THEIR FATHERS

(*Percentages*)

Group	Executives	Fathers
1900	62.0	72.7
1925	33.9	63.4
1950	16.6	63.5

[a] Entrepreneurs have been defined to include farmers and to exclude corporation officials except for those who founded their own corporations or bought control in a going concern. They include all who have had any independent business experience.

The preceding comparisons are made on the basis of the father's occupation at the time his son was started on his own career; if the father had more than one occupation at the same time, only his principal occupation is taken into account. However, a separate tabulation has been made of those fathers who at some time in their careers were in control of their own enterprise, whether a farm or some other type of business. This is shown in Table 21.

It is to be expected that there will be fewer men with independent business experience among executives than among their fathers, since the positions the executives hold are—except in the increasingly rare cases where the founder of the business is still in control —not those of independent businessmen. It is also to be expected that the proportion will decline with the decline of individual enterprisers among the United States population as a whole. It is surprising to find, however, that this same decline is not found among the fathers. The decline in men of independent business experience among the fathers of the 1925 group, as compared with 1900, is much smaller than that among the executives themselves, and there is no decline whatever between 1925 and 1950.[6] Nearly two-thirds of today's business executives are the sons of men with independent business experience, although only one in six has had such experience himself.

FAMILY INCOME

The family income, which is usually dependent on the father's occupation, is sure to play an important part in launching the sons on their careers. Adequate income facilitates the process of getting the necessary schooling and usually leads to influential connections. Also, it can provide the capital that is necessary for a new business enterprise or the acquisition of a going concern.

In the absence of actual income data, the classification of families according to income becomes a matter of judgment, and judgment based on rather meager information. The classification used—poor, medium, and wealthy—depends on a variety of criteria. In those instances where biographical data beyond that provided in *Who's Who in America* have been found, the biographer often states that the family was poor, rich, or middle class. These judgments are not always reliable, however, and have been checked wherever possible by other factors. Biographers appear to have a bias in favor of poverty, perhaps because this adds to the achievements of their subjects. Often, one of the best tests is the father's occupation. The family of the banker or capitalist has been assumed to be wealthy, unless he

---

[6] The reasons for this persistence of entrepreneurs among the fathers can only be conjectured. It seems probable that the business was sufficiently remunerative to make it possible to give the son the necessary education but not successful enough to encourage him to follow his father's occupation. And with the business tradition, the salaried corporation job offers the closest feasible alternative.

lost his fortune when his son was still a boy, and the family of the unskilled laborer has been assumed to be poor. When the father is a farmer or merchant or minister, however, further data are needed. The boy's own first job is sometimes an indication. The fact that he begins as office boy at a fairly early age is not in itself evidence of poverty; but if he quits school at thirteen to support a widowed mother, it has been assumed that the family was poor, regardless of the father's occupation. If he attended private school and college, and perhaps enjoyed a year of travel after that, it has been assumed that he was wealthy. For a few of the earlier executives the Census records of the value of the home gave the information needed.

The wealthy group is not assumed to have great wealth but to have some capital and to be accepted as wealthy in the community in which they live. The poor group is assumed to be unable to contribute to the son's education beyond the public school level or even to support him without any contribution on his part during his high-school course. If there is any marked change in family status, that prevailing at the beginning of the son's career is the one that has been used.

The distribution of families among these three classes is given in Table 22. It shows a disproportionate number of wealthy families as compared with the population of the United States as a whole. This is to be expected in view of the nature of this group. There is no important change in the proportion of poor in the three periods, but there has been a marked decline in the proportion of wealthy with a corresponding increase in the proportion of the middle income group among the 1950 executives as compared with those of 1900.[7] These data, it should be noted, apply to the period when the current executives were boys, and consequently precede the depression, highly progressive income taxes, and other changes that may have made inroads on the resources of the top income group. The change is probably due to the fact that, with the greater age of the corpora-

[7] The proportions for the 1900 group should be roughly comparable to those given by Miller ("American Historians and the Business Elite," *Journal of Economic History*, IX, No. 2 [November, 1949], 206), since there is a substantial overlapping in the two groups (100 of his 190 cases). Actually, Miller classifies 50 percent of his group as wealthy and only 5 percent as poor. The difference may be because of the inclusion in his group of a large number of banking and insurance executives, or it may be a difference in the standard by which wealth has been judged.

TABLE 22

FAMILY STATUS OF EXECUTIVES

(Percentage distribution)

Kind of Business	1900			1925			1950		
	Poor	*Medium*	*Wealthy*	*Poor*	*Medium*	*Wealthy*	*Poor*	*Medium*	*Wealthy*
Railroad	16.2	46.7	37.1	23.9	52.2	23.9	11.0	56.0	33.0
Public utility	17.3	29.3	53.4	19.2	40.4	40.4	9.0	64.4	26.5
Industrial	7.5	43.9	48.6	12.3	48.3	39.4	13.1	47.5	39.4
All kinds	12.3	42.1	45.6	15.8	47.8	36.3	12.1	51.8	36.1
Size of Corporation [a]									
Small	9.4	38.3	52.3	12.0	46.4	41.6	8.6	50.0	41.4
Medium	12.4	40.0	47.6	19.8	50.0	30.2	11.7	51.2	37.1
Large	17.1	51.3	31.6	16.0	46.9	37.1	14.1	50.7	35.1
Largest	…	…	…	…	…	…	16.4	57.5	26.1

[a] Classification by assets is shown in the following table:

CLASSIFICATION	ASSETS IN MILLIONS OF DOLLARS		
	1900	1925	1950
Small	40 or less	80 or less	100 or less
Medium	41–100	81–250	101–200
Large	101 or more	251 or more	201–500
Largest	…	…	501 or more

tions themselves, the way to the top is increasingly by working up from the bottom, and this route is open to all, provided a suitable education can be obtained.

A comparison of the proportions of executives from wealthy and poor families in corporations of different sizes reveals marked differences. Both in the 1900 group and the 1950 group the largest proportion of wealthy men is in the smallest corporations and the smallest proportion in the largest corporations. And the poor group increases correspondingly as the size of the corporation increases. In other words, the top positions in the largest corporations appear to be more readily available to the poor than the top positions in the smallest. The explanation lies primarily in the greater degree of inheritance in the smaller corporations. The really big corporations are too big to be inherited.[8]

TABLE 23

MEDIAN AGE OF REACHING POSITION AS CHIEF EXECUTIVE
IN RELATION TO FAMILY INCOME

	1900	1925	1950
Poor	51	50	50
Medium	49	48	53
Wealthy	45	48	49

Another interesting change is in the relation between the time it takes to get to the top and the wealth of the families from which the executives come. This is shown in Table 23. For the 1900 group it took the executives from poor families six years longer to reach the top, on the average, than the wealthy group. For the 1950 group it also took the poor longer, on the average, to reach the top, but the differential between the wealthy and the poor groups had narrowed to just one year. Again the evidence points to the fact that the advantage of the wealthy group has diminished as compared with fifty years ago.

[8] This same trend is noted by Stuart Adams in his study, "Trends in Occupational Origins of Business Leaders," *American Sociological Review*, XIX, No. 5 (October, 1954), 545. The proportion of business leaders from upper occupational groups increases from small to medium-sized businesses and then declines with the very large business. Mr. Adams's index is for occupational status of fathers rather than income, but the two are closely related. The historic decline in the proportion of leaders from upper-class families is also noted by Adams (p. 547).

CHAPTER SIX

EDUCATION OF EXECUTIVES

If education is oftentimes taken for granted by the business class, it is no exaggeration to say that it evokes the fervor of a religion, a means of salvation, among a large section of the working class.

R. S. AND H. M. LYND

THE importance of formal education in achieving economic advancement later in life is generally accepted. This attitude is clearly reflected in the Lynds' report on education in Middletown in the nineteen-twenties, a period when many of today's executives were still in school. It is summarized in the quotation given above. Parents are usually prepared to make real sacrifices to get their children through high school, at least. And regardless of parental wishes, the age of compulsory schooling has been advanced steadily. There is disagreement as to the most useful *kind* of education, and as to the number of years that should be devoted to it, but that a substantial amount of formal schooling is a business asset is not questioned. Parents and children may have a variety of ends in view when a college education is planned, but the probability of meeting influential people and improving job opportunities is rarely ignored.

HOW SHOULD BUSINESS EXECUTIVES BE EDUCATED?

The "professionalization of business executives" is recognized both in recent studies of the executives and the executive function [1] and in the establishment of graduate schools of business administration. But there is still a difference of opinion among the executives themselves as to the appropriate education for the profession and even as to the desirability of college or university training of any kind.

The quotation at the head of this chapter is taken from R. S. Lynd and H. M. Lynd, *Middletown*, New York: Harcourt, 1929, p. 187.

[1] See, e.g., R. A. Gordon, *Business Leadership in the Large Corporation*, Chap. XIV.

A generation or more ago most of the businessmen expressing themselves on this subject were of the belief that the best training was on the job and that a college education was a waste of time, at best, and might even prove a handicap. Henry Clews, for instance, wrote:

Therefore, I say to all who have sons destined for a business career, let your cherished offspring have the advantage of early practical training in the particular line of business for which you may consider them best adapted, and do so, even to the partial neglect of their school and college education. Practical business is the best school and college in which they can possibly graduate.[2]

He even goes so far as to say that a college education "is in many instances not only a hindrance, but absolutely fatal to success."[3] And Robert S. Bradley, former chairman of the board of American Agricultural Chemical and himself a Harvard graduate, is quoted by Barron as saying: "The trouble with Harvard University is that a man is not taught to do anything thoroughly. He is taught to 'get by' on his exams and then to forget. When he starts in business, if anybody will hire him, he has no value and it is difficult to teach him work and thoroughness."[4] Even today some heads of large corporations can be found who question the usefulness of a college education. However, the great majority of contemporary business executives appear to favor higher education. This is demonstrated both by what they say and by the competition among the large corporations for the best of each year's graduates.

The question under debate today is not so much the usefulness of higher education for the future executive as the kind of education. Some favor the liberal-arts training. H. W. Prentis, Jr., board chairman of Armstrong Cork, argues for a *liberal* education, stating that although business administration is becoming a profession, it requires more than mere specialized training.[5] Harry A. Bullis, board chairman of General Mills, is quoted as saying: "The education I had was

[2] Henry Clews, *Fifty Years in Wall Street,* New York: Irving Publishing Co., 1908, p. 37.

[3] *Ibid.,* p. 27.

[4] C. W. Barron, *They Told Barron,* New York: Harper, 1930, p. 298.

[5] H. W. Prentis, Jr., "Liberal Education for Business and Industry," *Bulletin of the American Association of University Professors,* XXXVIII, No. 3 (Autumn, 1952), 350.

the most important thing in my life. I hate to see education becoming more and more specialized. We can't have enough of the liberal arts." [6] And Irving Olds, former board chairman of United States Steel, is reported as saying: "The most difficult problems American enterprise faces today are neither scientific nor technical, but lie chiefly in the realm of what is embraced in a liberal arts education." [7] The Harvard Graduate School of Business Administration accepts this point of view insofar as its only formal requirement for admission is a bachelor's degree. Yet the same *Fortune* article quoted above points out that the corporation representatives recruiting on the college campuses show little interest in the liberal-arts graduates. Only 16 out of 117 interviewers at Yale in 1952 mentioned the possibility of using liberal-arts graduates, and at Johns Hopkins in 1952–53 this figure was 16 out of 200. Of the others, 145 wanted engineers, and 39 wanted other kinds of specialists. [8]

The undergraduate offerings in business administration at most universities leave the student little opportunity, if he majors in business administration, for a liberal-arts education. And the proportion of students getting their first degrees in a primarily liberal-arts course is steadily declining. [9] In another issue of *Fortune* it is stated that among the 1954 graduates are approximately 35,000 who have specialized in business and commerce courses at the collegiate level, as compared with 32,000 graduates in the humanities and the arts. [10] Moreover, the School of Industrial Management at Massachusetts Institute of Technology is open only to graduates who have majored in science or engineering.

It is, of course, recognized that the business schools are not designed exclusively to train top executives and that the 32,000 graduates in humanities and the arts might provide a good many executives for the top-flight corporations. But if the corporations themselves recruit primarily from graduates in engineering and business administration, and then select their executives from within, and if

[6] Leo Cherne, "Harry A. Bullis," *Saturday Review*, January 23, 1954, p. 25.
[7] "Should a Business Man Be Educated?" *Fortune*, XLVII, No. 4 (April, 1953), 114.
[8] *Ibid.*, p. 113.
[9] Less than one-third of recent male graduates, according to *Fortune, ibid.*, p. 114.
[10] Duncan Norton-Taylor, "The Business Schools: Pass or Flunk," *Fortune*, XLIX, No. 6 (June, 1954), 112.

graduate schools in business administration accept only students who
have majored in science or engineering, then there is little chance
either that the young man interested in a business career will select
a liberal-arts course in the first place, or that the corporation in search
of a president will find many liberal-arts graduates among its vice
presidents.

EDUCATIONAL EXPERIENCE OF TOP EXECUTIVES

The data of this study cannot provide any final answer to this
controversy. They do, however, show what the formal education of
the top executives has been, and they show marked changes in this
formal education over the period covered.

TABLE 24

EDUCATION OF CORPORATION EXECUTIVES [a]

(*Percentage distribution*)

Highest Level of Education Reached [b]	1900		1925		1950	
	Older	Younger	Older	Younger	Older	Younger
Grammar school	25.3	22.7	26.0	19.8	6.5	2.5
High school	35.4	38.0	24.4	27.5	24.3	16.8
College: no degree	10.1	11.4	12.6	10.6	11.8	14.8
College: 1st degree	24.0	17.9	26.0	25.1	44.8	45.8
Graduate school	5.1	10.0	11.0	17.0	12.6	20.1
	100.0	100.0	100.0	100.0	100.0	100.0
Number of cases included	79	231	119	207	382	487
Education unknown	1	5	. . .	4	6	7

[a] The younger group for 1900 and 1950 are those who had been in office less than
ten years as of the closing of the samples 1903 and 1953 respectively. The younger
group for 1925 are those who had been in office less than ten years as of the opening
date of the sample, 1923. The longer period allowed for the middle period was
chosen because of the smaller number of recent appointees in this period.

[b] Those attending business schools have been listed with the high school group.

The increase in the amount of formal schooling from one period to
the next is given in Table 24. This shows that the period of formal
schooling has increased steadily from the older to the younger appointees. Two out of five of the older 1900 executives had some college education as compared with four out of five of the younger 1950

executives.[11] The relatively high percentage of those not reaching high school among the older 1925 executives as compared with the younger 1900 executives is due primarily to the larger proportion of wealthy families represented by the latter group of executives. Even so the proportion of college-trained executives in the older 1925 group is much larger than that in the younger 1900 group.

Higher degrees are mainly in law and engineering. One M.D. is found among the 1950 executives, and Ph.D.s numbered 3 in the 1925 group and 9 in the 1950 group. There were 19 higher degrees in business administration in the 1950 group, 13 of them from Harvard.

TABLE 25

COMPARISON OF PROPORTION OF EXECUTIVES WITH SOME COLLEGE
EDUCATION AND PROPORTION OF TOTAL MALE POPULATION,
AGES 18–21, ENROLLED IN COLLEGES [a]

TOTAL MALE POPULATION		EXECUTIVES	
Year [b]	Percentage of College Enrollment	Group	Percentage Having Had Some College Education
1870	4.6	1900	39.4
1890	4.7	1925	51.4
1910	6.2	1950	75.6

[a] Computed from census data and data in *Biennial Survey of Education*.
[b] The year used for comparison is the census year nearest that for which the median age of the executive group was twenty.

The proportion of executives who have attended college is high in comparison with the proportion of the total United States population attending college in each of the three periods surveyed. In view of the wide variation in the ages of the executives within each group, only a rough comparison can be made to show this. This has been done in Table 25 by comparing the college attendance of the executives with the proportion of the male population from eighteen to twenty-one enrolled in college in the census years 1870, 1890, and 1910. These are the census years nearest the year in which the median age of the executive group was twenty.

The data in Table 25 show that even for the oldest group of executives the proportion that attended college was between eight and

---

[11] The older group are those holding a top executive position before 1894 and the younger group are those appointed 1944 or later.

ten times that for the male population of their generation. Also, the proportion of college-educated men among the executives increased somewhat faster than the proportion for the male population as a whole, so that for the youngest group the proportion who attended college is approximately twelve times that for their generation.[12]

The self-made man whose formal education did not extend beyond grammar school has almost disappeared. However, the proportion of business executives with some higher education is smaller than that for distinguished persons as a whole, as listed in *Who's Who in America*. Taussig and Joslyn's comparison shows that 45.3 percent of their business leaders had some college education, whereas the corresponding percentage for the persons listed in *Who's Who* for that period was 77.4.[13] The 1925 group of the present study, which represents much the same period as the Taussig study, shows 51.4 percent of the top business executives with some college training. Extending this comparison to the current generation, we find that the proportion of persons listed in *Who's Who in America* for 1952/53 with some higher education has risen to 92.5 as compared with 75.6 percent for 1950 executives.[14] The business executives still fall behind the average education of all individuals listed in *Who's Who*, but the difference is narrowing. Moreover, the average age of the 1950 business executives probably was a little higher than that of the individuals listed in *Who's Who*. The percentage of the more recent business executives with some higher education is 80.7.

[12] Other studies that include businessmen of earlier periods also show a higher proportion of college-educated among business leaders than among the population as a whole, although the proportion of college men is smaller in the earlier samples of businessmen. Keller shows 35 percent of the business leaders of 1870 with some college education (S. I. Keller, "The Social Origins and Career Lines of American Business Leaders," New York: Columbia University, 1953, Ph.D. thesis, unpublished, p. 73); and Mills, whose study covers even earlier periods, notes that in each period the educational background of the business group is far above the average for their contemporaries (C. Wright Mills, "The American Business Elite: a Collective Portrait," *Journal of Economic History*, Supplement V [1945], p. 34.)

[13] F. W. Taussig and C. S. Joslyn, *American Business Leaders*, New York: Macmillan, 1932, p. 162.

[14] The percentage for *Who's Who* was obtained by tabulating education of individuals listed on five consecutive pages for each letter of the alphabet. The reliability of the sample was tested by computing the percentage for the first and second halves separately. No appreciable difference was found for the two halves. The total number of cases was 2,004.

EDUCATION IN RELATION TO SIZE OF CORPORATION
AND KIND OF BUSINESS

The education of executives varies somewhat according to the size of corporations and the type of business they engage in. For the 1925 executives the proportion of college-trained officers is higher in the large companies than in the small ones (see Table 26). This checks with the findings of Taussig and Joslyn, who conclude that the larger the business the greater the number of college-educated executives.[15] The relationship between size of business and degree of education extends through all five of the size groups in the Taussig study. The great majority of the corporations in the present study fall in Taussig's largest group.[16]

The same relationship does not appear in the 1900 and 1950 data, except that the proportion of officials with graduate training increases with size in these periods also. But any such tendency in the group with only undergraduate college training is blurred by the fact that undergraduate training is more common in wealthy families, and executives from wealthy families are found in greater proportion among the smaller corporation executives. Even when the executives from wealthy families are excluded from the tabulation, however, the tendency is not marked.[17] The detailed comparisons of education by corporation size are given in Table 26.

Marked differences appear in the kind and amount of education when the executives are classified according to the business of their corporation. Table 27 shows that the proportion of officials who have had some college education is greater among the public utilities than among either the railroads or the industrial corporations. These also have a larger proportion of officers with engineering degrees in 1950, although not in the earlier periods, and a relatively large propor-

[15] Taussig and Joslyn, *American Business Leaders*, pp. 181–82.
[16] Since gross receipts were used in the one study to measure size, and assets in the other, exact comparisons are not possible.
[17] For 1950, 67.5 percent of executives from middle- and low-income families had some college training in the two groups of smaller corporations, as compared with 70.8 percent in the two groups of larger corporations, but the principal difference is in the very large corporations. In these, more than 80 percent of the executives who have come from middle- and low-income families have some college training.

tion of officers with law degrees. The railroad executives included a much larger proportion of college men in 1900 than the industrials, but the rapid increase in the number of college men among the industrials over this period has brought the percentage of college executives in this group far ahead of the percentage of college executives in the railroad group. This increase in college education among the

TABLE 26

EDUCATION OF EXECUTIVES IN RELATION TO SIZE OF CORPORATION

(*Percentage distribution*)

Assets in Millions of Dollars	Number of Officers	Grammar and High School	College: Undergraduate	College: Graduate	Total
1900					
40 and under	127	61.1	35.7	3.2	100.0
41–100	107	56.6	32.1	11.3	100.0
Over 100	76	68.5	17.1	14.4	100.0
1925					
80 and under	128	54.6	35.9	9.4	100.0
81–250	117	46.2	36.7	17.1	100.0
Over 250	81	42.0	38.2	19.8	100.0
1950					
100 and under	272	22.0	66.2	11.8	100.0
101–200	248	27.0	57.6	15.4	100.0
201–500	210	28.6	46.6	24.8	100.0
Over 500	139	18.0	64.8	17.2	100.0

industrial executives is not due primarily to the growth in professional degrees. The railroad executives still outrank the industrial executives in the proportion of engineering and law degrees, and the proportion of law degrees among the industrial executives actually declined slightly between the 1925 and 1950 periods.

THE EDUCATIONAL INSTITUTIONS AND PROFESSIONAL TRAINING

The universities most frequently attended by the executives are listed below (Table 28), together with the number of top executives educated in each. The total number of institutions represented are 51 in 1900, 92 in 1925, and 170 in 1950. The "Ivy League" holds no monopoly. One-third of the degrees of the 1950 group come from

TABLE 27

COLLEGE EDUCATION OF OFFICERS IN DIFFERENT TYPES OF BUSINESS

(Percentage distribution)

TYPE OF BUSINESS	SOME COLLEGE EDUCATION WITH OR WITHOUT DEGREES			WITH COLLEGE DEGREES			WITH ENGINEERING DEGREES			WITH LAW DEGREES		
	1900	1925	1950	1900	1925	1950	1900	1925	1950	1900	1925	1950
Railroad	42.9	49.2	67.7	30.5	39.1	51.6	10.5	20.2	20.4	9.5	10.1	12.9
Public utility	45.8	63.0	78.9	35.1	46.3	66.1	3.5	16.7	33.9	12.3	11.2	13.8
Industrial	34.2	49.2	75.8	23.5	38.9	62.5	5.3	9.8	15.8	6.0	12.3	11.1
All [a]	39.3	51.5	75.6	28.3	40.2	62.1	6.8 [b]	13.2 [b]	20.0 [b]	8.4 [c]	12.0 [c]	11.9 [c]

[a] Number of cases included in percentages above: 310 for 1900; 326 for 1925; 869 for 1950. No information was available for, respectively, 6, 4, and 13 officers.

[b] Graduate and undergraduate. The percentages for graduate degrees alone in the three periods are 2.9, 4.6, and 4.7, respectively.

[c] Graduate and undergraduate. The percentages for graduate degrees alone in the three periods are 4.9, 8.0, and 6.1, respectively. Graduate study includes LL.B.'s if these require more than a four-year university course, where this information was available. Since the degrees were obtained in different periods and law-school requirements have changed, this could not always be determined.

state and municipal institutions, as compared with one-sixth from these institutions among the 1900 group. There is no question as to the social prestige of such institutions as Harvard, Yale, and Princeton. But Harvard's law school and school of business administration and Yale's engineering school are largely responsible for their top-ranking positions.

TABLE 28

PRINCIPAL UNIVERSITIES AND NUMBER OF EXECUTIVES ATTENDING EACH [a]

1900		*1925*		*1950*	
Institution	*Number of Executives*	*Institution*	*Number of Executives*	*Institution*	*Number of Executives*
Harvard	22	Columbia	18	Harvard	74
Yale	12	MIT	14	Yale	62
Columbia	10	Harvard	13	Princeton	34
MIT	5	Yale	12	Cornell	33
Michigan	4	Princeton	10	Michigan	31
		Lehigh	8	Columbia	29
		Michigan	6	MIT	23
		Amherst	5	Wisconsin	17
				Pennsylvania	15
				California	14

[a] If one executive attended two institutions, both were counted.

No information has been obtained concerning the number of executives who specialized in business administration during their undergraduate course. However, a recent *Fortune* survey of a group of business executives closely paralleling those of the 1950 group in the present study shows that 38.5 percent of the top executives under fifty who have had college training specialized in business economics.[18] This compares with 28.9 percent specializing in science and engineering, 16.9 percent in law, and 12 percent in the arts. The same study shows that the proportion specializing in science and engineering is much higher for executives over fifty than for the younger group, whereas the proportions specializing in the other areas have increased for the younger executives.

Graduate study in business administration has not been generally

[18] "The Nine Hundred," *Fortune*, XLVI, No. 5 (November, 1952), 135. The *Fortune* executives included the three highest-paid in each of the largest corporations (250 industrials, 25 railroads, and 25 public utilities).

available, even to the 1950 generation, and consequently graduate degrees in business administration are few. The only graduate school of business in which any appreciable number of these executives has been trained is the Harvard School of Business Administration. Thirteen of the 1950 executives attended this school. While this is less than 2 percent of the total group of executives, it must be remembered that this school was extremely small until the late nineteen-twenties, and the great majority of the 1950 executives had completed their formal education before that time. It may be that in the future graduate training in business administration will become as essential in top business positions as graduate training has become in law.[19] Certainly, such training is one of the tests of a profession.

EDUCATION AND FAMILY STATUS

The relation of family status to the extent of formal education is very marked, as is to be expected. This is shown in Table 29. Among the 1900 group no member of the executives from poor families got beyond high school, although more than half of the wealthy group had some college education. Even for the 1925 group less than one in ten of those from poor families got as far as college, although seven out of ten of those from wealthy families reached college. For the 1950 group, however, half of those from poor families reached college, and while by that time 90 percent of those from wealthy families had some college education, the gap between the two groups is not so wide as it was fifty years earlier. If those members of the 1950 group that have been appointed in the period since 1943 are tabulated by themselves, it appears that two-thirds (35 out of 53) of those from poor families have some college education. It seems to be increasingly true that a college education is becoming a prerequisite for top positions and that, at the same time, the way to the top is open to men from poor families once the necessary education is obtained.

[19] Although there are still very few graduate schools of business administration in the country, most universities offer some graduate work in this field. In 1952 the number of advanced degrees in commerce and business was 3,914 as compared with 4,620 advanced degrees in engineering (*Statistical Abstract of the United States*).

TABLE 29

FAMILY STATUS AND EDUCATION OF CORPORATION EXECUTIVES [a]

(Percentage distribution)

Highest Level of Education Reached	1900			1925			1950		
	Poor	Medium	Wealthy	Poor	Medium	Wealthy	Poor	Medium	Wealthy
Grammar school	71.1	27.3	6.4	78.4	18.3	2.6	23.8	3.0	...
High school	21.1	40.6	39.0	13.7	28.1	27.6	25.7	23.5	10.0
College: no degree	7.8	7.8	14.8	3.9	9.8	16.4	11.9	13.3	15.6
College: 1st degree	...	13.3	30.5	3.9	26.8	34.5	32.7	42.3	54.1
Graduate study	...	11.0	9.2	...	17.0	19.0	5.9	17.9	20.3
	100.0	100.0	100.0	100.0	100.0	100.0	100.0	100.0	100.0

[a] The percentages are based on 307 cases in 1900, 320 cases in 1925, and 832 cases in 1950; for all these information was available concerning both family status and education. No information was available for 9 executives in 1900, 10 in 1925, and 50 in 1950.

The tendency of the wealthy families in the 1900 group to send their sons to college appears to have been motivated more by social custom or the fact that education in general was regarded as "a good thing" than by the idea of training them specifically for the family business. It is true that some of the Guggenheims attended schools of mining, and some of the du Ponts were students of chemistry. Also, the study of law was frequent. But in most instances the education had no obvious business motive. Very few of those from middle- and lower-income families reached college, and there is no indication that a college education was regarded by them as in any way a stepping stone to advancement toward an executive post. The biographies of the earlier executives often explain the interruption of the individual's schooling as being for "reasons of health," although he might enter the family business immediately without an intervening period of recuperation. Formal education, in other words, was not a very serious pursuit. This differentiates the earlier group from the 1950 generation rather sharply. Today it is accepted that the college degree is the ticket of admission to a successful career with the large corporation even though the initial employment for the college graduate may be manual labor.

EDUCATION AS A SHORTCUT TO PROMOTION

One of the questions often raised is whether higher education is the shortest as well as the surest route to the top. The data of Table 30 throw some light on this question. In both 1900 and 1950 the median age of reaching the top position was lowest for the nonengineering group graduating from college but not continuing their studies. In 1925 those with engineering degrees (mostly first degrees) were on the average one year younger than the others with first degrees, but both of these groups were younger than either those who did not reach college, at one end of the scale, or those who pursued graduate study, at the other end.

This is to be accounted for in part, but not entirely, by the fact that the wealthy group both advances more rapidly than the others and is more likely to obtain a college education. However, when the wealthy are excluded from the tabulation of the first-degree group,

Table 30

Median Age of Attaining Top Executive Position, by Family Status and Highest Level of Education Reached

(Figures represent age at which top position was attained)

Family Status	All Educational Levels	Grammar School	High School	College: No Degree	First Degree[a]	Graduate Study[a]	Engineering Degree
1900							
Wealthy	45	53	46	40	44	46	46
Medium and poor	49	51	49	51	47	49	50
All	48	51	48	46	45½	46	46
1925							
Wealthy	48	50	49½	49	43	45	49
Medium and poor	49	51	48	49	51½	48	44
All	49	51	48	49	46	48	45
1950							
Wealthy	49	...	53	52	48	48	47
Medium and poor	52	53	54	53	51	52	55
All	52	53	53	52	50	51	52

[a] Excluding engineering degrees.

its members still reach the top a little sooner than the others for the 1900 and 1950 executives, although not for the 1925 executives. In no period is the differential very great, but it seems safe to conclude that the time spent on higher education has not, by delaying their start in the business world, also delayed their arrival. And for the 1950 group it appears to have advanced the time of final promotion slightly. The smaller number of cases in the earlier periods, especially in the middle- and lower-income groups, makes the differentials found in these periods less reliable.

Table 31 summarizes the comparisons between the college-educated and the noncollege groups, showing the age at which the top was reached by those with and without a college education, and those from wealthy and from poor and middle-income families.

TABLE 31

MEDIAN AGE OF ATTAINING TOP EXECUTIVE POSITION IN RELATION TO FAMILY STATUS AND COLLEGE EDUCATION

(The figures represent the age at which top position was attained)

	POOR AND MEDIUM INCOME GROUP		WEALTHY GROUP	
	No College Education	*Some College Education*	*No College Education*	*Some College Education*
1900	50	49	47½	43
1925	50	48	50	46
1950	54	52	51	48

EDUCATION IN RELATION TO THE WAY IN WHICH THE TOP
POSITION WAS OBTAINED

There is a marked relationship between the level of education and the manner of reaching the top. Table 32 shows that the grammar-school group includes a higher proportion of executives who founded their own businesses than any other group in each of the three periods. Thirty-four percent of the grammar-school executives in the 1900 group organized their own companies, as compared with 30 percent for all levels of education. And while this proportion dropped to 19 percent for the grammar-school executives in 1950, it dropped to 6 percent for all executives.

Those who inherited their positions have more than their propor-

Table 32

Relation of Education to Way in Which Top Position Was Obtained

Principal Factor in Obtaining Office	All Educational Levels	Grammar School	High School	College: No Degree	First Degree	Graduate Study	Engineering Degree[a]
1900							
Work in organizing company	29.5	33.8	32.7	31.4	23.5	14.8	33.3
Inheritance	5.5	...	6.2	14.3	8.5	3.9	...
Investment	19.5	16.9	22.1	14.3	25.5	14.8	16.7
Success in another company	13.6	18.3	13.3	2.9	17.0	14.8	8.3
Working up within company	17.9	21.1	15.9	25.7	10.6	18.5	16.7
Other	14.0	9.9	9.7	11.4	14.9	33.3	25.0
	100.0	100.0	100.0	100.0	100.0	100.0	100.0
1925							
Work in organizing company	16.3	23.9	15.5	11.4	16.4	10.6	14.8
Inheritance	14.1	4.2	15.5	17.1	27.3	10.6	7.4
Investment	14.4	14.1	17.9	8.6	20.0	8.5	11.1
Success in another company	11.9	12.7	9.5	8.6	10.9	14.9	18.5
Working up within company	37.4	39.4	35.7	45.7	20.0	46.8	48.1
Other	6.0	5.6	5.9	8.6	5.5	8.5	...
	100.0	100.0	100.0	100.0	100.0	100.0	100.0
1950							
Work in organizing company	6.0	19.4	12.8	6.4	1.2	5.2	3.9
Inheritance	13.8	2.8	6.1	18.2	22.6	11.9	7.8
Investment	7.0	5.5	3.0	10.0	10.5	5.2	3.9
Success in another company	18.2	8.3	13.4	13.6	20.6	17.0	28.7
Working up within company	50.8	50.0	62.2	46.4	41.9	53.3	54.3
Other	4.2	13.9	2.4	5.5	3.2	7.4	1.5
	100.0	100.0	100.0	100.0	100.0	100.0	100.0

a Graduate and undergraduate.

tionate share of men with B.A. degrees, as is to be expected from the fact that they come almost exclusively from wealthy families. Those with specialized degrees, on the other hand, whether under-graduate engineering or graduate degrees of any kind, contain rela-tively few men who arrived either through inheritance or investment. The holders of specialized degrees worked up within the company more often than those with a general college education, with or without the first degree. In fact, in 1950 only the high-school group has a larger proportion of those that worked up from the bottom than the specialized degree holders, and in 1925 no group had a larger proportion of those working up than the holders of specialized degrees. In the 1950 group, executives who have been chosen be-cause of success in another company turn up in larger proportion among the men with higher degrees than among those who did not graduate from college or even reach it. This is not true, however, of the earlier periods.

EDUCATION OF EXECUTIVES IN RELATION TO CORPORATE GROWTH

While the foregoing data show the extent of education among corporation executives and differences for different periods and dif-ferent classes of corporations, they can give no indication of what type of education makes the most successful executive. One ap-proach to this problem that can be made from the data available is to compare the education of the executives of rapidly growing cor-porations with that of executives of corporations that are growing slowly or actually declining. The test of growth used—change in assets between 1924 and 1949—leaves something to be desired; and even if this were to be accepted as completely satisfactory, it would have to be conceded that growth or lack of growth is determined by many factors outside the control of the chief executives, however well or poorly qualified they may be. Moreover, it can always be de-bated what is cause and what effect.[20] Nevertheless, the comparison is believed to be useful. It is limited to 109 executives of industrial corporations the assets of which increased five times or more in the period selected, and to 144 executives of industrial corporations the

[20] Other differences in these two groups of corporations are noted on pp. 138–39.

assets of which did not double in this period. Twenty-two of these latter officials were heads of corporations the assets of which decreased. If allowance is made for changes in purchasing power of the dollar in this period, all these "slow-growing" companies were static at best. The comparison is shown in Table 33.

TABLE 33

COMPARISON OF EDUCATION OF EXECUTIVES IN FAST-GROWING
AND SLOW-GROWING COMPANIES, 1950

	NUMBER OF EXECUTIVES		PERCENTAGE OF EXECUTIVES	
EDUCATION	*Fast-Growing Companies*	*Slow-Growing Companies*	*Fast-Growing Companies*	*Slow-Growing Companies*
No college	28	34	25.7	23.6
Undergraduate	70	84	64.2	58.3
Graduate	11	26	10.1	18.1
Law degrees [a]	10	22	9.2	15.3
Engineering degrees [a]	9	19	8.3	13.2
Total	109	144	100.0	100.0

[a] First and advanced.

The slow-growing corporations have a larger proportion of executives with graduate training than the fast-growing corporations. Most of the graduate training was in engineering and law. Also, the proportion of executives with engineering and law degrees—including both first and higher degrees—is larger among the slow-growing than among the fast-growing corporations.[21] These data appear to give some support to the contention that the best training for chief executives is a liberal arts course.

[21] See p. 138 for further comparisons of the education of these two groups of officers.

CHAPTER SEVEN

EARLY BUSINESS CAREER

A family's position in the prestige structure is recognized locally as an important factor in the determination of who gets what job, no matter where the family is in the structure or where the job is in the economic system.

A. B. HOLLINSHEAD

FAMILY ASSISTANCE IN GETTING STARTED

IN addition to educating their sons, families often participate directly in launching them on their business careers—taking them into the family business, providing the necessary capital, or persuading friends and acquaintances to take them into their businesses. For those executives whose biographies are fairly extensive, the first job and how it was obtained is usually recorded in the biographies. For those whose biographical data are limited to *Who's Who in America*, there is no direct information on the way in which the job was obtained, and only when it was in the family business was it possible to trace family influence. Consequently, the data that follow probably understate the extent of family assistance. The evidence is sufficient in enough cases, however, to reflect the general trends for this period as well as differences for corporations of different sizes and for different kinds of business.

Table 34 shows that the proportion of individuals starting in the family business and later becoming chief executives in this business increased in the second period, as compared with the first, and then declined in the third. The explanation of this is that the majority of corporations in the first period were less than ten years old, whereas by 1925 the majority had been established long enough for

The quotation at the head of this chapter is taken from A. B. Hollinshead, *Elmtown's Youth*, New York: Wiley, 1949, p. 363.

the presidency to be inherited from an older generation. If it is assumed that inheritance is possible only in those companies that had had a life of at least twenty years by 1900, 1925, and 1950 respectively, then the percentage of those who might have inherited their positions and actually did so was 30 percent in 1900, 23 percent in 1925, and 15 percent in 1950.

TABLE 34

FAMILY ASSISTANCE IN BUSINESS CAREER

	NUMBER OF EXECUTIVES			PERCENTAGE OF EXECUTIVES		
	1900	1925	1950	1900	1925	1950
First job [a]	79	53	98	25.6	16.3	11.5
Corporation office [b]	27	61	121	8.7	19.0	14.2
Financial aid [c]	26	21	16	8.4	6.5	1.9
No direct aid [d]	177	188	616	57.3	58.2	72.4
Total	309	323	851	100.0	100.0	100.0
No information	7	7	31			

[a] Position in another business or minor position in the corporation of which he became chief executive. To illustrate, one railroad president's father was station agent for the railroad of which his son became president and started his son as a telegraph operator for the railroad. Another was shop foreman and employed his son as a manual worker under him. Those first employed by the father's friends are also included in this group. Only full-time jobs are included. Part-time and summer work during schooling has been ignored.

[b] Father or other close relative held important executive post in corporation of which this officer became president or board chairman.

[c] This includes neither financial aid in obtaining an education nor small gifts. Where the individual inherited office as well as capital, he has been included in the corporation office group. Where he received a substantial inheritance but did not use it directly to obtain office in this corporation, he appears under one of the other classifications.

[d] This includes all who did not obtain either their first position or the presidency directly from relatives in the business or from money received from the family.

The proportion receiving substantial financial aid from the family, or direct aid in obtaining the first position, has also declined sharply; and the proportion receiving no direct assistance from the family has increased correspondingly.

In Table 35 the officials have been grouped according to the type of business and size of corporation. This shows a decrease in the proportions receiving family assistance in obtaining their first jobs in every group. But it also shows that a much larger proportion of the industrial executives than the railroad and public utility executives received such aid. These differences are due partly, but not entirely, to the fact that the industrials are on the average somewhat smaller than the railroads and public utilities. The executives of the largest corporations received direct family assistance in obtaining their first jobs far less frequently than the executives of the smallest corporations. However, for the corporations with assets in excess of $500,000,000, only one-tenth of the railroad executives had received direct aid from their families as compared with one-fourth of the industrial executives of the 1950 group. And among the smallest corporations of the 1950 generation, inheritance is likewise much more frequent among the industrial than the railroad and public utility officials.

TABLE 35

PERCENTAGE OF EXECUTIVES RECEIVING DIRECT AID FROM
THEIR FAMILIES IN OBTAINING THEIR FIRST JOB

	1900	1925	1950
Railroads	33.3	23.9	19.3
Public utilities	37.9	40.4	12.9
Industrials	51.4	48.0	33.2
Smallest corporations [a]	46.9	45.8	29.6
Largest corporation [b]	30.3	29.6	18.2

[a] Assets $40,000,000 or less in 1900, $80,000,000 or less in 1925, and $100,000,000 or less in 1950.
[b] Assets over $100,000,000 in 1900, over $250,000,000 in 1925, and over $500,000,-000 in 1950.

For all groups of executives, family assistance increasingly takes the form of providing a college education, and perhaps professional training at the graduate level, rather than capital or a place in the family business or the business of some friend. The contacts made at college, whether through chance acquaintance or through corporation agents sent to the campuses in search of promising candidates for jobs, increasingly supply the channels through which the first opportunity is obtained. The widespread use of "talent scouts" by the corporations is a comparatively new development, and most of the 1950 executives obtained their first jobs in other ways. Rarely was one of the members of the 1950 group offered a job before he left the college campus. The job seekers were expected to take the initiative, and did so. College and university placement bureaus might assist, but there was no accepted procedure, and much was left to chance. One picked his company and applied in person. Another answered a newspaper advertisement. Still another heard of a vacancy through a friend. One was unable to find any work in the field of his choice. Another succeeded in getting the kind of work he wanted only after a year of hunting. Lawyer fathers might take their lawyer sons into partnership; but many—and particularly the engineers— were seeking positions in fields with which their fathers had little contact. Even those whose families appear to have been in a position to help them often preferred to seek their own position, confident that their skills were marketable. And since most were well launched before the depression of the thirties, they usually met with early success.

Many of the first jobs were humble enough, but starting at the bottom is regarded more and more as good experience. Even the heirs were more likely to have served an apprenticeship at manual labor that was more than a token service than those of earlier generations. And for those making their own way, almost any job brought "contacts" and an opportunity to prove worth; and promotion to more suitable posts came in due course.

FIRST FULL-TIME POSITION

Turning from the way in which the first full-time job was obtained to the nature of the job itself, Table 36 gives the distribution of these positions for the three periods. The largest group for all three periods is that of clerical and minor administrative positions. But this has declined in recent years, whereas the different professional groups are increasing. All professions combined accounted for 23 percent of the first positions among the 1900 executives and 38 percent among the 1950 executives. The largest number of professional jobs are in engineering. This is also one of the fastest growing groups. The legal positions are second in importance, but the proportion of these has remained fairly constant. The proportion of those who started their careers as independent businessmen has never been large and is declining.

The average age at which the first position was obtained necessarily rises with the prolonging of education. The number of executives who left school and started in their full-time business activi-

TABLE 36

FIRST FULL-TIME POSITION OF EXECUTIVES

	NUMBER OF EXECUTIVES			PERCENTAGE OF EXECUTIVES		
POSITION	1900	1925	1950	1900	1925	1950
Independent business	10	9	16	3.4	2.9	1.9
Corporation official a	16	21	61	5.4	6.8	7.3
Clerical and minor administrative	104	96	195	34.9	30.9	23.5
Skilled labor	25	36	65	8.4	11.6	7.8
Unskilled labor	19	23	42	6.4	7.4	5.1
Errand boy b	20	24	52	6.7	7.7	6.3
Salesman c	35	19	83	11.8	6.1	10.0
Engineer	23	38	139	7.7	12.2	16.8
Lawyer	28	33	85	9.4	10.6	10.2
Accountant	. . .	1	23	. . .	.3	2.8
Other professions	18	11	69	5.9	3.5	8.3
Total	298	311	830	100.0	100.0	100.0
No information	18	19	52			

a Most of these were in corporations headed by some member of the family. The positions are those ordinarily included in the corporation's published list of officials, and not minor officials.

b This includes office boys, messengers, delivery boys, etc. Many more held such positions on a part-time basis during their school years.

c This includes salesmen in retail stores, traveling salesmen, and members of sales departments of corporations.

ties before twenty is shown in Table 37 as far as the exact age of starting has been found. This shows both a sharp decline in the percentage of those who went to work before they were twenty and an increase in the median age of beginning for the group who went to work young. The percentage of executives known to have started before twenty decreases from 40 for the year 1900 to 18 for 1950. If it is assumed that all those who did not attend college started work before twenty and none of those who attended college started work before twenty (and this is approximately what does take place), the proportion of executives beginning their business careers before they reached twenty was about three out of five in 1900, as compared with something less than one in four in the 1950 group.

The youngest full-time workers appear to have been T. W. Hall of American Hide and Leather, who was hired out to a farmer at the age of eight and had no schooling after that time, and C. W. Nash of Nash Motors, who was also apprenticed to a farmer at the

TABLE 37

AGE OF BEGINNING FULL-TIME WORK FOR THOSE EXECUTIVES
WHO STARTED BEFORE TWENTY [a]

| | | NUMBER OF OFFICERS | |
AGE	1900	1925	1950
7	. . .	1	1
8	1	. . .	. . .
9	2	. . .	1
10	. . .	. . .	. . .
11	4	1	2
12	4	4	5
13	12	10	5
14	20	20	8
15	20	9	19
16	20	20	28
17	10	19	33
18	14	19	32
19	18	13	20
Total under 20	125	116	154
Percentage starting before 20	39.6	35.2	17.5
Median age of beginning for those under 20	15	16	17

[a] These ages represent the age of beginning full-time work. Summer jobs or part-time jobs during the school year are not included.

age of six or seven (the biographies differ as to his exact age) and received very little schooling of any kind. Most of the very young were apprentices or office boys or messengers, but the group under twenty include 35 heads of independent businesses and 29 school teachers. It also includes some who were not only self-supporting but without guardians. Mr. Nash ran away from the farm where he was apprenticed at the age of twelve or thirteen and obtained a position as a farm hand with wages. Another, according to a letter from a relative, left home at fourteen because of a disagreement with his parents and was completely self-supporting and independent from that time on. Others not only undertook to support themselves but members of their families as well. Several obtained full-time work at thirteen or fourteen to support their widowed mothers. This, of course, is no longer possible. Compulsory education and welfare laws prevent it. If the widowed mother is unable to support her son today, she will receive aid for dependent children. And the boy who runs away from home will be returned there or provided with a responsible guardian.

PRINCIPAL OCCUPATIONS

The first full-time job has not usually been one that has led directly to the top, although the number of executives whose total business experience is limited to the corporation they finally headed is fairly large.[1] In an attempt to ascertain the principal channels through which these men finally reached the top executive position, they have been classified according to their principal occupational experience. Professional men have been classified as such if they practiced their profession at any time. A man with legal training who went directly into business without serving as legal counsel has not been classified as a lawyer, but if he practiced law at some time or held a position as legal officer of a company, he has been classified as a lawyer even though he later became, say, a capitalist. Capitalists are those who obtained their office by large investments in the company and who neither organized it nor had any professional status. Those who both organized and financed their own businesses are classified as entrepreneurs. Bankers and brokers include both independent businessmen and the principal officers of banking corporations. The salaried administrators are those who have no professional status and who have held wage and salaried positions throughout their business careers, even though they may, as president or board chairman, exercise as much control over the corporation as those who established it in the first place or those who bought a

[1] For further discussion of this, see pp. 97–98.

controlling share of the stock. The distribution of executives among different occupations for the three periods is shown in Tables 38 and 39.

TABLE 38

PRINCIPAL OCCUPATIONAL EXPERIENCE OF EXECUTIVES

	NUMBER OF EXECUTIVES			PERCENTAGE OF EXECUTIVES		
OCCUPATION	1900	1925	1950	1900	1925	1950
Entrepreneur [a]	97	66	86	31.0	20.2	9.9
Capitalist [b]	39	20	43	12.5	6.1	4.9
Banker or broker [c]	24	12	43	7.7	3.7	4.9
Engineer	39	51	168	12.5	15.6	19.3
Lawyer	41	45	104	13.1	13.8	11.9
Other professions [d]	12	9	69	3.8	2.7	7.9
Salaried administrator	61	123	358	19.5	37.7	41.1
Total	313	326	871	100.0	100.0	100.0
No information	3	4	11			

[a] Many of these might be classified as capitalists. These, however, have established and operated independent businesses at some time, whereas the capitalists have only invested in or inherited going concerns.

[b] Thirty-five of the 43 capitalists of 1950 inherited the office and the investment from other members of the family, whereas in 1900 this was true for only 11 of the 39 capitalists.

[c] The brokers numbered 4 in 1900, 1 in 1925, and 5 in 1950.

[d] Includes scientists, physicians, army and navy officers, accountants, and those with degrees from graduate schools of business administration.

TABLE 39

PRINCIPAL OCCUPATIONAL EXPERIENCE OF EXECUTIVES, BY EARLIER AND LATER APPOINTEES

(Percentage distribution)

	1900		1925		1950	
Occupation	Earlier	Later	Earlier	Later	Earlier	Later
Entrepreneur	27.5	32.2	25.4	17.3	15.3	5.6
Banker and capitalist	23.8	18.9	9.3	10.1	13.5	7.0
Engineer	8.8	13.6	17.8	14.4	17.9	20.4
Lawyer	13.8	12.9	9.3	16.3	10.4	13.2
Other professional	4.9	3.4	2.5	2.9	4.1	10.8
Salaried administrator	21.2	18.9	35.7	38.9	38.7	43.0
	100.0	100.0	100.0	100.0	100.0	100.0

The most striking change in the principal occupational experience of the executives between 1900 and 1925 is in the rapid increase of salaried administrators. These are the men who have never run a business of their own, do not own a controlling share of "their" corporation, and do not belong to the professional group as that term is ordinarily understood. They have learned on the job, and while they have taken no prescribed course and have no degrees to prove it, they may well be regarded as professional administrators.[2] This group increased more slowly in the second twenty-five-year period than the first. However, the percentage of salaried administrators rises from 30 in 1900 to 56 in 1925 and to 72 in 1950 if we include among salaried administrators all those executives with professional training who have never carried on an independent practice or headed their own business enterprise and all those investors who have inherited office but do not have a large enough investment to give them control. The last period showed a large increase in the salaried professional group.

Among the professional men, regardless of whether they have engaged in independent practice or have served only as salaried corporation officials, the engineers and lawyers predominate. However, there has been a marked increase in the engineers during this fifty-year period, whereas the proportion of lawyers has declined slightly. When the 1950 group is divided into those appointed in 1944 or later and those appointed before 1944, the increase in the professional group among the younger men is very marked, reaching 44 percent of the total. The percentage of engineers in the younger group rose to 20, and that of the lawyers rose from 10 percent for the earlier appointees to 13 percent for the later appointees.

The entrepreneurs have declined markedly, and among the later 1950 appointees they are less than 6 percent of the total. Bankers and capitalists also have declined steadily, falling to only 7 percent of the later 1950 appointees.

The occupational distribution of the executives for different kinds of business and for different sizes of corporations is shown in Tables 40 and 41. The industrial corporations have more entrepreneurs and fewer engineers than the railroads and public utilities; and except for

[2] Some, of course, have had undergraduate business courses.

TABLE 40

PRINCIPAL OCCUPATIONAL EXPERIENCE OF EXECUTIVES IN DIFFERENT TYPES OF BUSINESS

(Percentage distribution)

Occupation	1900			1925			1950		
	Railroad	Public Utility	Industrial	Railroad	Public Utility	Industrial	Railroad	Public Utility	Industrial
Entrepreneur	14.3	22.4	46.0	2.9	25.0	24.9	6.6	5.1	11.8
Banker and capitalist	19.0	27.6	18.0	13.0	13.4	7.8	7.5	2.8	12.4
Engineer	16.2	12.1	10.0	26.1	25.0	9.7	22.6	40.1	12.6
Lawyer	20.0	12.1	8.7	13.0	13.5	14.1	9.7	15.3	11.3
Other professions	...	...	8.0	...	3.8	3.4	4.2	6.8	8.8
Salaried administrator	30.5	25.9	9.3	45.0	19.4	40.0	49.5	29.9	43.1
	100.0	100.0	100.0	100.0	100.0	100.0	100.0	100.0	100.0

TABLE 41

PRINCIPAL OCCUPATIONAL EXPERIENCE OF EXECUTIVES IN CORPORATIONS OF DIFFERENT SIZES

(Percentage distribution according to assets in millions of dollars)

Occupation	1900			1925			1950			
	Assets 40 or Less	Assets 41–100	Assets over 100	Assets 80 or Less	Assets 81–250	Assets over 250	Assets 100 or Less	Assets 101–200	Assets 201–500	Assets over 500
Entrepreneur	37.2	32.4	18.4	31.2	16.2	8.6	9.6	14.0	9.0	4.3
Banker and capitalist	22.4	17.6	19.7	10.1	10.2	8.6	9.9	10.0	7.1	13.7
Professional	31.1	28.6	27.6	25.0	35.0	39.5	34.9	31.7	44.4	52.5
Salaried administrator	9.3	21.3	34.2	33.6	38.5	43.2	45.6	44.4	39.5	29.5
	100.0	100.0	100.0	100.0	100.0	100.0	100.0	100.0	100.0	100.0

1900 the public utilities have fewer unspecialized salaried administrators than either the railroads or the industrials. Bankers and capitalists were formerly found in largest proportions in the railroad
and public utility corporations. In 1950 they were more frequent
among the industrial executives.

The percentage distribution of the different occupations varies
even more when the executives are classified by size of corporation
rather than by kind of business. The greatest differences appear in
the percentages of entrepreneurs, which decrease as the size of the

TABLE 42

EXECUTIVES WITH INDEPENDENT BUSINESS OR PROFESSIONAL EXPERIENCE

	1900		1925		1950	
Experience	Older	Younger	Older	Younger	Older	Younger
	NUMBER OF EXECUTIVES					
Independent business [a]	53	141	50	57	92	53
Independent profession [b]	7	18	7	29	39	58
Neither	20	74	61	122	254	375
Total	80	233	118	208	385	486
No information		3	1	3	3	8
	PERCENTAGE OF EXECUTIVES					
Independent business	66.2	60.6	42.4	27.4	23.9	10.9
Independent profession	8.7	7.7	5.9	13.9	10.1	11.9
Neither	25.0	31.6	51.7	58.7	66.0	77.2
	100.0	100.0	100.0	100.0	100.0	100.0

[a] Includes all who conducted and controlled a business (corporation or other) at any
time in their business careers. This includes, in the case of the corporations, those who
participated in the organization of a new business or who had sufficient investment in a
going concern to give them control.
[b] Mostly lawyers with private practice, but includes independent engineers, accountants, and other professional men.

corporation increases, and in the percentages of professional men,
which—except in the 1900 group—increase with size. Although the
great majority of nonprofessional salaried administrators were found
in the large corporations in 1900, the reverse was true in 1950. The
salaried administrator in the large corporation today tends to be a
professional man.

Two final points of interest in connection with the occupational
experience of the chief executives are the proportion of those who

have at some time been independent business or professional men and the proportion of those who have always held a wage or salaried position. These are shown in Table 42. The change in the independent professional group has not been large during this period, but the proportion of those with independent business experience has declined from two-thirds to approximately one-tenth of the total, and those who have always been on salaries have increased from one-fourth to more than three-fourths. It is recognized that many of these salaried officers have very real control of their corporations. But they do not have large investments in them, and their incomes bear little relation to the profits of the business.

CHAPTER EIGHT

THE
CHIEF EXECUTIVES' SERVICE
IN THEIR OWN CORPORATIONS

We recently started to give a lot of attention to the hiring of office boys. We have suddenly waked up to the fact that office boys have a way of growing up to be contenders for the presidency.

A CORPORATION PRESIDENT

THE executives of 1900 were working in a period when "big business" was developing very rapidly. As noted earlier, half of the business concerns included in this study had been in existence ten years or less. This meant that a large number of the executives were the first to head their companies. They had no accepted procedures to follow, no trained staff to carry on the business, and no predecessors to advise them. Whatever the advantages or disadvantages of such a situation, it demands different skills and presumably offers greater risks than the administration of a well-established and successful going concern.

Among the 1900 group of executives, two out of five were the first presidents or board chairmen of their companies. Among the industrials this was true for three out of five. For the 1925 executives, only one in eight was a "first" top executive, and among the 1950 group these were only one in twenty-five.

The quotation at the head of this chapter is taken from J. Elliott Janney, "Company Presidents Look at Their Successors," *Harvard Business Review*, XXXII, No. 5 (September–October, 1954), 49.

LENGTH OF SERVICE WITH COMPANY BEFORE

ATTAINING PRESIDENCY

In view of the youth of the companies themselves, there was little opportunity for the 1900 group of executives to have gained experience from long periods of service with their corporations. More than half of this group of executives had never worked for the corporations they headed except as many of them were themselves the organizers of the enterprise. This is in sharp contrast to the situation today. Only 23 percent of the 1950 executives came from outside the corporation, and less than 20 percent of the more recent appointees of this group came from outside. The great majority of the 1950 group had some previous service with their corporations, and the service for most of them was fairly long. Three-fifths of them had been with the company more than 10 years when they became chief executive. This is shown in Table 43. The median years of service before reaching the top was 16 years, and for the more recent appointees of this group 19 years. One reached the top position only after 52 years of service with his company.

TABLE 43

LENGTH OF EMPLOYMENT WITH CORPORATION BEFORE
BECOMING PRESIDENT OR BOARD CHAIRMAN [a]

YEARS OF EMPLOYMENT	NUMBER OF EXECUTIVES			PERCENTAGE OF EXECUTIVES		
	1900	*1925*	*1950*	*1900*	*1925*	*1950*
None	186	102	201	59.2	30.9	22.9
1–10	69	90	151	22.0	27.3	17.2
11–20	30	59	163	9.6	17.9	18.6
21–30	16	46	199	5.1	13.9	22.7
Over 30	13	33	162	4.1	10.0	18.5
Total	314	330	876	100.0	100.0	100.0
No information	2	. . .	6			

[a] The median length of employment was "none" for the 1900 executives, 7.5 years for the 1925 executives, and 16 years for the 1950 executives.

The average length of service for the 1950 group before the presidency is shortest for the public utility executives and longest for the industrial executives. However, promotion is slowest in the railroads. The average length of service is shorter for the railroads than for the industrials because the railroads select their top officials from outside the company more frequently than the industrials. The median length of service prior to the presidency, in the 1950 group, for those coming up within the company is 20 years for the public utilities, 21 years for the industrials, and 25 years for the railroads. The median for the three groups is 21 years, and for the recent appointees 23 years.

TABLE 44

PERCENTAGE OF EXECUTIVES WITH BUSINESS EXPERIENCE
LIMITED TO THEIR OWN COMPANY

Factors in obtaining office	1900	1925	1950
Founders	1.1	3.8	8.0
Inheritors	94.1	93.5	77.2
Executives who worked up	7.3	15.8	29.0
Type of business			
Railroad	4.8	7.2	20.9
Public utility	5.3	9.6	11.3
Industrial	8.6	27.1	30.6
All executives	6.8	20.0	22.1

Not only have the majority of executives of the 1950 group had long service with their companies before reaching the top; a large proportion of them have had their entire business experience with their own companies. The proportion with no outside business experience is shown in Table 44. The increase in the numbers with no outside experience between the 1900 and 1925 groups is largely to be explained by the increased length of life of the corporations. The smaller increase in the proportion whose business experience is limited to their own company among the 1950 executives as compared with those of 1925 is due primarily to the decline in inheritance. It is to be expected that those who inherit the family business will normally start with the family company. It is true that the proportion of inheritors with no outside experience has declined over the period studied, but it was still 77 percent in the 1950 group. At the same time, among those reaching the top by long service the number who have had no outside experience, although much smaller than among the inheriting group, increased from 16 to 29 percent between 1925 and 1950. These data are given in Table 44. This increase in the proportion of those working up within the corporation who have had no experience with another business concern can be explained only on the assumption that long service with the company is increasingly recognized as a qualification for leadership. There has been no increase in the average length of life of the corporations themselves in this period that can account for this.

The proportion of officers with no outside experience is highest among the industrial corporations, largely because of the greater amount of inheritance in this group. However, the small percentage of public utility officials with no outside experience, as compared with the railroad officials, is not to be explained in this way, since the number of inheritors is very small in both these groups.[1]

The average number of years of service is longest for the heirs and for those who work up within the corporation. These two groups normally spend most of their working lives with the same corporation. The heirs, on the average, have 21 years of service to their credit before reaching the top. Several waited more than 40 years for promotion, and one waited 50 years. A vice presidency may come early, but there are often more sons than presidencies and chairmanships, and the father may himself remain in office until he is eighty or more.

Those who work up without benefit of family wait a little longer— 25 years on the average instead of 21. Eleven of this group served more than 45 years before reaching the presidency. One attained it, as noted earlier, only after 52 years of service. The corporation itself discourages shifting from one company to another. Most of the private pension systems and stock options available to junior executives lose all or most of their value when the individual leaves the company. At the same time the lengthening period of service within the company has created some uneasiness on the part of the authorities on executive qualifications.

In most of the discussions of the kind of experience that is desirable for a top executive a broad experience is emphasized. To illus-

[1] See Table 44.

trate, McMurry says: "The kind of person who has the patience and submissiveness to be content for the major portion of his career to remain as second or third man in an organization is not inherently an entrepreneur." [2] And further: "A man habituated for years to thinking almost exclusively, for example, in terms of sales or production will experience great difficulty, in spite of his honest efforts to the contrary, in reorienting his thinking to see the whole operation in balanced perspective. Almost inevitably he will find himself seeing the organization's problems primarily from the perspective of his old specialty." [3] And J. B. Sheridan:

We are raising a lot of thoroughly drilled "yes ma'ms" in the big corporations, who have no minds of their own; no opinions. As soon as the old individualists die, and there are not so many of them left, I think the corporations will have a lot of trouble in getting good executives. After a man has served 20 to 30 years in one of these monstrous corporations he is not liable to have much mind of his own. [4]

In practice, however, there appears to be little effort to seek outside talent. Rather, the corporations are attempting to achieve the necessary perspective and breadth by sending some of their best executives to university training programs for executives.

PRINCIPAL FACTORS IN OBTAINING EXECUTIVE OFFICE

Any attempt to trace the way in which office was obtained must take into account first such factors as family influence, financial control, and individual initiative and effort. Second, it is important to trace the channels through which the individual has risen within the corporation, both the departments and the specific offices.

The principal factors that have been responsible for the attainment of a top executive position have been classified as (1) work in organizing a corporation, (2) inheritance, (3) investment, (4) success in another company, (5) working up within a company, and (6) all other factors. It is obvious that more than one of these factors may operate in individual cases and this makes any classification

[2] R. N. McMurry, "Man-Hunt for Top Executives," *Harvard Business Review*, XXXII, No. 1 (January–February, 1954), 59.

[3] *Ibid.*, pp. 58–59.

[4] Director of Missouri Committee on Public Utility Information in a letter quoted in Carl D. Thompson, *Confessions of the Power Trust*, New York: Dutton, 1932, pp. 14–15.

somewhat arbitrary even when the information concerning the individual is fairly complete. The resulting grouping of individuals has all the limitations of a value judgment based on inadequate data, but it is believed that even with these limitations it throws some light on the relative importance of the various factors in the different periods under consideration.

When an individual organizes his own enterprise and heads it, the way he came into office is clear. When he is a member of a group launching a new enterprise, he may be chosen because he is the principal promoter behind the enterprise, because he has provided most of the capital, or because he is adjudged the ablest administrator. Ordinarily the individual who became president after participating in the organization of a corporation has been classified in the first group regardless of the specific contribution he may have made to it. All who were preceded in office by relatives have been classified as inheritors, although many have worked up within the company in a very real sense and have had to demonstrate administrative ability as well as put in long years of apprenticeship before reaching the top.

The category of "investment" has been reserved for those who neither participated in the organization of the company nor were preceded in office by other members of the family. They have made substantial investments in the corporation after it was organized and are presumably the largest single investors in the company if not the owners of a majority of the shares of stock. Or they are the representatives of the owners. Those who were chosen for "success in another company" are men who had demonstrated administrative ability in high office in other companies and had no close connection with the company that selected them. Most were presidents of similar but smaller companies. Some were vice presidents of other similar companies, and some came from quite different kinds of business. Most had no experience with the company itself, but if an individual was brought into the company at the vice-presidential level and promoted to president within a year or two, it has been assumed that he was brought in with prompt promotion in mind, and he has been included in this group.

"Working up within the company" is applied to all with no relatives in high office before them and who have several years of service (usually five or more), some promotion within the company, and no important investment. Most of those included in the "all other" group were officials of subsidiaries at the time of consolidation, with neither special merit or large investment clearly demonstrated. A few of this group have had other kinds of connections with the company they headed—as suppliers, as customers, or as agents for special and temporary activities. Presumably the members of this group were chosen largely on merit, but there was not the same degree of competition that appears to prevail for the group chosen from unrelated companies. They fall somewhere between those who have worked up within the company and those who have demonstrated success in another company.

The proportions falling in these different categories are given in Table 45. This shows clearly the decline in the number of organizers and investors and the great increase in the number promoted from within. There has been some decrease in the proportion of those inheriting office in recent years—a substantial decrease if allowance is made for the growing opportunity for inheritance.[5] And there has been some increase in the proportion chosen for success in another company. In short, two-thirds of the 1950 executives appear to have been selected for personal achievement either within their own company or in another company, as compared with less than one-third in the 1900 group. They are administrators rather than innovators and risk takers.

The proportion chosen for success in other companies, while increasing, is still small in view of the emphasis placed by authorities on the qualifications for business leadership on the desirability of breadth of experience and the importance of having had actual responsibility for making important decisions. This implies that successful executives in other business concerns are likely to be better qualified for the job than second-ranking executives within the corporation. In spite of this, nearly three times as many executives were chosen from officials who had worked up within the company as were chosen from outside. Some of these, of course, had had a good deal of independence as the chief executives of subsidiaries, but most

[5] See discussion above, pp. 83–84.

were merely vice presidents in charge of some specialized department of the corporation.

TABLE 45

PRINCIPAL FACTORS IN OBTAINING EXECUTIVE OFFICE

	NUMBER OF EXECUTIVES			PERCENTAGE OF EXECUTIVES		
PRINCIPAL FACTOR	1900	1925	1950	1900	1925	1950
Work in organizing corporation	92	52	50	29.5	16.3	6.0
Inheritance	17	45	114	5.5	14.1	13.8
Investment	60	46	58	19.5	14.4	7.0
Success in another company	42	38	151	13.6	11.9	18.2
Working up within company	55	120	421	17.9	37.4	50.8
Other	43	19	35	14.0	6.0	4.2
Total	309	320	829	100.0	100.0	100.0
No information	7	10	53			

Tables 46 and 47 show the principal factors in obtaining executive office for the railroads, public utilities, and industrials separately for 1950, and for all corporations for 1950 broken down by size of corporation. The most striking differences among the three types of corporation are the comparatively small proportion of in-

TABLE 46

PRINCIPAL FACTORS IN OBTAINING EXECUTIVE OFFICE FOR
1950 OFFICIALS, BY TYPE OF BUSINESS

	NUMBER OF EXECUTIVES			PERCENTAGE OF EXECUTIVES		
		Public			Public	
PRINCIPAL FACTORS	Railroad	Utility	Industrial	Railroad	Utility	Industrial
Work in organizing corporation	. . .	9	41	. . .	5.7	7.1
Inheritance	4	6	104	4.4	3.8	18.0
Investment	14	10	34	15.5	6.3	5.9
Success in another company	27	42	82	29.7	26.4	14.2
Working up within company	46	82	293	50.5	51.6	50.6
Other	. . .	10	25	. . .	6.3	4.2
Total	91	159	579	100.0	100.0	100.0
No information	2	23	28			

TABLE 47

PRINCIPAL FACTORS IN OBTAINING EXECUTIVE OFFICE FOR 1950 OFFICIALS, BY SIZE OF CORPORATION

(Assets in millions of dollars)

PRINCIPAL FACTORS	NUMBER OF OFFICIALS				PERCENTAGE OF OFFICIALS			
	Assets 100 or Less	Assets 101–200	Assets 201–500	Assets over 500	Assets 100 or Less	Assets 101–200	Assets 201–500	Assets over 500
Work in organizing corporation	17	20	10	3	6.6	8.4	5.1	2.1
Inheritance	41	42	22	9	16.0	17.5	11.1	6.6
Investment	18	17	18	5	7.0	7.0	9.1	3.7
Success in another company	55	48	30	18	21.5	20.1	15.1	13.2
Working up within company	115	105	104	97	44.9	43.9	52.5	71.3
Other	10	7	14	4	3.9	2.9	7.1	2.9
Total	256	239	198	136	100.0	100.0	100.0	100.0
No information	19	18	13	3				

dustrial executives taken from outside concerns and the larger proportion of inheritors in this group. Investors are most frequently found among the railroad executives. All three groups are obtaining approximately half of their chief executives from within.

Analyzing the factors by size of corporation, the most important difference is the increase in the proportion of executives who have worked up within the company as the size of the corporation increases, with a correspondingly smaller proportion of executives from all other sources. Whether this is due primarily to the fact that the large corporations have more administrative talent to select from or to other factors is not clear. It is not wholly the result of the larger number of investors and inheritors in the smaller companies, since the proportion chosen for success in other companies also declines in the larger corporations.

TABLE 48

OUTSTANDING VOTING STOCK OWNED BY EXECUTIVES IN THEIR
OWN CORPORATIONS, 1952, BY SIZE OF CORPORATION [a]

(Assets in millions of dollars)

	PERCENTAGE OF EXECUTIVES				
PERCENTAGE OF STOCK HELD	*All Corporations*	*Assets 100 or Less*	*Assets 101–200*	*Assets 201–500*	*Assets Over 500*
None	2.1	3.7	0.9	2.6	0.7
Less than 0.1	48.8	26.6	43.8	56.3	82.7
0.1–1.0	32.0	41.6	36.3	30.2	12.0
1.1–5.0	11.0	19.6	11.4	5.7	3.8
5.1–10.0	3.0	3.3	5.4	1.6	0.8
10.1–25.0	2.0	3.3	1.8	2.1	. . .
25.1–50.0	0.8	1.9	0.4	0.5	. . .
Over 50.0	0.3	. . .	. . .	1.0	. . .
	100.0	100.0	100.0	100.0	100.0
Number of cases	765	214	226	192	133
No information [b]	117	61	31	19	6

[a] Compiled from data in notices of annual stockholders' meetings.
[b] These include very recent appointees and executives of corporations in which stock is closely held.

Taking the executives as a whole, the proportion that apparently obtained office through investment has declined. Exact data on the stockholdings of the chief executives are not available for the two earlier periods, but the number of shares held is, of course, regularly reported today in the notices of stockholders' meetings for all corporations with widely distributed stock ownership. And these data are given for the 1950 group of executives in Tables 48 and 49.

TABLE 49

PROPORTION OF OUTSTANDING VOTING STOCK OWNED BY EXECUTIVES
IN THEIR OWN CORPORATIONS, 1952, BY TYPE OF BUSINESS
AND LENGTH OF SERVICE [a]

	TYPE OF BUSINESS			LENGTH OF SERVICE OF APPOINTEES	
PERCENTAGE OF STOCK HELD	Railroad	Public Utility	Industrial	Over 10 Years	10 Years or Less
None	5.7	3.4	1.1	1.2	2.8
Less than 0.1	70.1	69.4	39.9	33.3	61.1
0.1–1.0	16.1	21.8	37.6	38.5	27.0
1.1–5.0	6.9	3.4	13.8	16.8	6.6
5.1–10.0	1.2	0.7	4.0	4.8	1.6
10.1–25.0	. . .	0.7	2.3	3.7	0.5
25.1–50.0	. . .	. . .	1.1	1.4	0.2
Over 50.0	. . .	0.7	0.2	0.3	0.2
	100.0	100.0	100.0	100.0	100.0
Number of cases	87	147	531	336	429
No information [b]	6	35	76	52	65

[a] Compiled from data in notices of annual stockholders' meetings.
[b] These include very recent appointees and executives of corporations in which stock is closely held.

The proportion of voting stock held by the executives, as shown in these tables, understates somewhat the number of large holdings since these appear in disproportionate numbers in the corporations in which stock is held by a small group of individuals, and holdings for these are not usually reported in notices of stockholders' meetings. However, the tables record the holdings of 87 percent of the executives, and some of the missing individuals are new appointees in corporations for which stocks are widely scattered. Consequently, when allowance is made for this bias in the record, it is still clear that the great majority of the officials hold less than 1 percent of the voting stock. They did not in the first place obtain their positions through their own legal control, and the authority with which the office endows them is dependent on the continuing approval of directors and stockholders. This also means that they are for the most part dependent on their salaries rather than on their dividends for their incomes, although dividends on 1 percent of the stock of a billion-dollar corporation can mount up to substantial sums.

Further analysis of the data in Table 48 shows that stockholdings are lowest in the largest corporations. In corporations with assets in excess of half a billion dollars, only 5 percent of the executives own as much as 1 percent of the stock of their corporations, whereas more than one-fourth of the executives in the smallest corporations own more than 1 percent of the stock. Comparison of the different kinds of business reveals the fact that executive stock ownership is higher among the industrial executives than among the railroad and public utility executives. And comparison of the earlier and later appointees shows a substantial decline in ownership in the latter group. This is partly because they tend to increase stockholdings over the years, stimulated by stock-participation plans and also, doubtless, assisted by their own growing income. It is also a reflection of the decline in the number who have achieved office by inheritance or investment and of the increase in the number who have worked up within the corporation. Even in the earlier group of appointees, however, only about 10 percent own as much as 5 percent of the stock of their corporations.

CORPORATE POSITIONS HELD PRIOR TO CHIEF EXECUTIVE OFFICE

The principal channels through which those that have worked up within the company eventually reached the top are given in Table 50 for 1925 and 1950. The group of 1900 executives who rose within the company is too small to make such a classification meaningful for them and consequently has not been included here. Some of these executives have had a widely varied experience within the company in the course of their service, but this has usually come at the beginning, when they had not yet found their proper niche, or at the end, after they had been chosen to succeed the president and were being trained by him for the succession. Most of the executives have clearly specialized in some division of the company through most of their service, and even as vice presidents are commonly labeled as specializing in sales, production, finance, or whatever department they head. In fact, it is common practice for each important department to be headed by a vice president. The group classified as "general" in Table 50 includes such officers as the assistant to the president and others not attached to any of the special divisions listed.

TABLE 50

DEPARTMENTS WITHIN CORPORATIONS THROUGH WHICH
EXECUTIVES REACHED TOP POSITION [a]

(Number of Executives)

	1925			1950		
Departments	Railroads and Public Utilities	Industrials	Total	Railroads and Public Utilities	Industrials	Total
Operations and production	28	23	51	70	105	175
Finance	5	7	12	15	57	72
Sales and advertising	...	11	11	3	55	58
Legal	9	13	22	16	32	48
Receivers	...	...	...	4	2	6
Personnel	...	...	...	...	1	1
General and other	6	10	16	7	16	23
Total	48	64	112	115	268	383
No information	4	4	8	13	25	38

[a] This includes only those executives who worked up within the corporation which they finally headed and does not include experience with other business concerns.

The earlier training of the officials is closely related to the offices they hold. The engineers have for the most part been engaged in operations or production, and the lawyers have served as general counsel or in the legal department. But the original specialty is less closely related to the particular office held as they rise to the top. The nonprofessional college graduates are more likely than the professional group to have engaged in sales and advertising or in finance, although most of the small group with graduate degrees in business administration are in these departments. And those without college degrees are found in disproportionate numbers in finance. Most of the noncollege group started as clerks, bookkeepers, and office boys. Very few started as manual laborers. The engineers appear to have more manual labor to their credit than those who did not get beyond the secondary schools.

There is little evidence to support the statement frequently made that the sales managers are more likely to succeed than the production managers. Although there are many outstanding executives in the 1950 group who have come up through sales, there are also some conspicuous failures among those who advanced from sales managers—and this was a period in which conspicuous failures were rare. Moreover, the growth of the professionally trained group—whose members are rarely found in sales departments—at the expense of the nonprofessional salaried administrator appears to contradict the belief that the sales managers are most likely to reach the top.[6] It cannot be assumed, on the other hand, that because the largest group has come up through operations and production that this is the surest road to the top, since there is probably a larger group of officials to draw on in the operations and production divisions than in the other branches. Executives selected from the sales and financial divisions increased in numbers more rapidly than those selected from the operations and legal divisions between 1925 and 1950. Whether this reflects a growing preference for this training or merely a larger group of officials to select from is not known.

There is good reason to believe that those close to the head office are more likely to be noticed and advanced than those more remote from headquarters. But vice presidents are usually chosen to represent each important division of the company, and in the end the president is usually selected from among the vice presidents. Of the 882 presidents and board chairmen in the 1950 group, 513 had previously been vice presidents of their companies. This is a much higher proportion than is found among the 1925 group, one-third of whom had served as vice presidents, or among the 1900 group, only one-sixth of whom had served as vice presidents. The difference is

[6] Only one in five of the sales group had any professional training, compared with nearly half of the operations and production group.

due in part to the greater number of the more recent executives chosen from within the company, and in part to the growing custom of giving vice-presidential rank to the important officials, such as the secretary, comptroller, treasurer, and general manager. The older corporations had no such galaxy of officers to select from. The officer finally chosen is often the executive vice president. In fact it is often assumed that the executive vice president when given this position has already been selected for the presidency. The data on vice presidents advanced to the chief executive offices are given in Table 51.

TABLE 51

FREQUENCY OF VICE-PRESIDENTIAL OFFICE AMONG EXECUTIVES AND AVERAGE LENGTH OF SERVICE AS VICE PRESIDENT

	1900	1925	1950
Percent of total who served as vice president	17.2	35.2	58.2
Percent of those promoted from within corporation who served as vice president	42.2	50.9	75.6
Median years of vice-presidential service	4	6	7

INFLUENCE OF CHIEF EXECUTIVES IN SELECTION OF SUCCESSORS

The foregoing data give some indication of the kind of training the executives have had and of the influences that appear to have operated in the final selection. The selection is made, however, by individuals who necessarily take into account a larger variety of factors than can be measured and who probably could not themselves state with any degree of conviction just why they have found one man rather than another best qualified for the job. Technically, the selection is made by the board of directors, but unless there is active board opposition to the outgoing executive, his recommendation for a successor will ordinarily be sought and approved. Often the chief executive selects his successor years in advance and trains him for the job. Assistants to the president often succeed them in office; but whether they were selected for succession before they became the presidents' assistants or whether their success as assistants was what placed them in the line of succession is not always clear, though instances of both can be found.[7] Some executives never squarely face the problem of replacement until the time arrives. This is not surprising in view of the fact that the executives themselves are usually expected to take the initiative, and they are not all prepared either to give up control or to take any steps toward that end.

When a chief executive officer dies while in office without having selected a successor, the board necessarily takes the initiative. A few other instances have been found where the initiative was taken by the board—or, in case of financial difficulties, the bankers—but without apparent opposition from the retiring officer. No instance has been found, although doubtless they occur, of the board going against the expressed wishes of the retiring officer.

Even when the recommendation comes from the executive officer, however, it is not necessarily a one-man decision. The recommendation may well be preceded by consultation with other officers, and particularly with directors. Even without formal consultation, the attitude of others in the organization must often influence the president's choice. But there is every indication that the final selection is usually made from a rather limited circle. Small corporations with a dearth of administrative talent sometimes make an extensive search for a new executive officer, even hiring experts to do the job for them. But the big corporations, with a large group of administrators of their own to draw on, tend to select from within. This is clear from the proportion of chief executives who were promoted from within, which increases, as shown in Table 47, as the size of the corporation increases.

[7] Specific instances of a president selecting his successor are as follows: Deupree of Procter and Gamble was selected for the presidency by W. C. Procter (*Fortune*, XLV, No. 5 [May, 1952], 134); Colbert of Chrysler was "hand-picked" by his predecessor Keller, now chairman, and trained for the job over a period of twenty years. Keller himself had been selected by Chrysler (*Fortune*, XLIX, No. 4 [April, 1954], 220). Gaugler of American Cyanimid was selected by his predecessor, Bell (*Fortune*, XLV, No. 6 [June, 1952], 124). And Cordiner of General Electric was the choice of C. E. Wilson, his predecessor, and worked with Wilson for some years before he became president (*Fortune*, XLV, No. 5 [May, 1952], 154). These were chosen from within the company. Colley of Atlantic Refining chose Supplee as his successor on the basis of his administration record in a milk company. He was brought to Atlantic Refining as a vice president several years in advance of promotion (*Fortune*, XLVIII, No. 2 [August, 1953], 128). Porter of National Distillers chose Bierwirth, a banker, as his successor (*Fortune*, XLVIII, No. 4 [October, 1953], 148). And Ferry, chairman of Packard, took Nance from General Electric to head Packard (*Fortune*, XLVI, No. 5 [November, 1952], 118).

AGE OF ATTAINING CHIEF EXECUTIVE OFFICE

The average age of reaching the presidency or board chairmanship has increased. The difference is not as great as the growing length of service with the company might lead one to expect, since this is compensated for in part by a decreased period of service in other business concerns. Nevertheless, the median age of attaining the top position has advanced from 48 for the 1900 executives to 52 for the 1950 executives. And when a comparison is made between the earlier appointees of the 1900 group and the later appointees of the 1950 group, the median age of appointment is found to have increased from 46 to 55. Moreover, the average length of service in the top position has increased so that the average age of the incumbents as of 1900 and 1950 respectively advanced from 53 to 61. These comparisons are given in Tables 52 and 53.

TABLE 52

AGE DISTRIBUTION OF CORPORATION EXECUTIVES,
FIRST YEAR OF OFFICE

AGE	NUMBER OF EXECUTIVES			PERCENTAGE OF EXECUTIVES		
	1900	1925	1950	1900	1925	1950
21–30	19	10	21	6.1	3.0	2.4
31–40	55	45	80	17.5	13.7	9.1
41–50	114	139	300	36.3	42.3	34.1
51–60	93	100	352	29.6	30.4	40.0
61–70	27	34	108	8.6	10.3	12.3
71–80	5	1	17	1.6	0.3	1.9
81 and over	1	. . .	1	0.3	. . .	0.1
	314	329	879	100.0	100.0	100.0
No information	2	1	3			

Table 54 also shows the differences in the age of attaining the top position as among the railroads, public utilities, and industrials as well as among corporations of different sizes. The railroad executives tend to attain the top office a little later than the public utility and industrial executives, and the heads of the largest corporations reach the top a little later than the heads of the smaller corporations.

The age of attaining the top position varies considerably with the way in which the office was attained. This is apparent in Table 55.

TABLE 53

RANGE OF EXECUTIVES' AGES, FIRST YEAR OF OFFICE
AND YEAR OF RECORD

	AGE IN FIRST YEAR OF OFFICE			AGE IN YEAR OF RECORD [a]		
RANGE	1900	1925	1950	1900	1925	1950
Youngest	21	24	23	26	31	33
First quartile	41	43	45	45	53	57
Median	48	49	52	53	58	61
Third quartile	54	55	57	60	64	67
Oldest	84	73	82	83	91	93

[a] These are computed from the ages of those actually in office in the year specified. The number of cases is: 1900, 192; 1925, 313; 1950, 686.

TABLE 54

MEDIAN AGE OF APPOINTMENTS TO OFFICE

	1900	1925	1950
All executives	48	49	52
Railroad	50	51	55
Public utility	46½	45½	52
Industrial	47	48	51
Smallest group	46	46	51
Largest group	50½	50	53
Earlier appointees	46	46	47
Later appointees	49	50	55

TABLE 55

MEDIAN AGE OF ATTAINING PRESIDENCY IN RELATION
TO WAY IN WHICH OFFICE WAS ATTAINED

Principal factor in Obtaining Office	1900	1925	1950
Work in organizing company	45	45½	43
Inheritance	38	45	45
Investment	48	51½	51
Success in another company	49	48	52
Working up within company	51	50	54
Other	49	51	49
Entire group	48	49	52

The youngest groups are those who organize their own business concerns and those who inherit office. In 1900 the inheritors were much the youngest group, but in 1950 the organizers were the youngest. And at the other end of the scale, the oldest group (except in 1925) is the group that worked up within the company.

One of the qualifications usually advanced for choosing a top administrator is that he should still be in his prime, and also young enough to have a reasonable term of office before retiring, in order to establish and carry out his policies. There is some agreement that a reasonable term is ten years or more.[8] Using ten years as a test, and sixty-five as a reasonable age of retirement, any candidate for promotion to a top executive post would be disqualified on the basis of age if he had passed his fifty-fifth birthday. That no such test is in fact generally applied is apparent from the above data. Half of the later appointees of the 1950 group had passed their fifty-fifth birthday at the time of promotion. This was also true of the railroad executives, early and recent appointees alike. And for all executives of the 1950 group, 315, or 36 percent,[9] had passed their fifty-fifth birthday when they were promoted, 57 had passed their sixty-fifth birthday, 21 had passed their seventieth birthday, and 3 had passed their eightieth birthday.

Most, but not all, of those past 70 when they obtained the top position were either large investors or held a chairmanship that did not carry with it the title of chief executive officer. But the same cannot be said for the group appointed in their sixties and late fifties. Comparatively few of these were on a semiretired basis. The great majority of those appointed after fifty-five have been chief executive officer, often president and chairman combined, who obtained the position, apparently, on merit or as a reward for long service. And the number of chief executive officers who relinquish this office at sixty-five, even when they shift from the presidency to the chairmanship, is comparatively small.

[8] See, *e.g.*, M. E. Dimock and H. K. Hyde, "Executive Appointment in Private and Public Bureaucracies," in R. K. Merton and others, *Reader in Bureaucracy*, Glencoe: Free Press, 1952, p. 324.

[9] When those younger men who went out of office before the end of ten years are added to this group, the proportion in office for not more than ten years before age 65 is well over half.

The data on age distribution do not bear out the belief frequently expressed that big business executives suffer from overwork and worry and die at a comparatively early age from heart failure or ulcers.[10] It is possible that this applies to the vice presidents, but in view of the relatively advanced age at which the final promotion is likely to occur, it seems probable that those who live long enough to reach the top are a comparatively hardy group. A comparison of the age distribution in 1950 of chief executives between sixty and seventy with the age distribution of the total white male population in their sixties in that year shows that the decline in the number of executives between sixty-five and sixty-nine as compared with the number between sixty and sixty-four was approximately the same as the decline in the total male population between these two age groups. Yet the total male population includes all those living, whether active or retired, whereas the executive group includes only those still in active service. It is true that the group of executives between sixty-five and sixty-nine includes some new appointees, but it is also true that retirements exceeded new appointments in this age group.

TERMS OF OFFICE AND TOTAL YEARS OF SERVICE

The terms of office as president, chairman of the board, or both are given in Table 56 so far as these are available. A small number of 1925 executives and most of the 1950 executives are still in office.

The 1900 executives were operating in a period of almost revolutionary change, with financial control shifting from group to group, new and larger combinations swallowing earlier large combinations, and numerous highly speculative ventures being launched only to fail completely at an early date. Consequently, terms of office were abnormally brief. The 1925 group, operating in a more settled period and directing older and better established businesses, had much longer tenure of office on the average. For the 1950 group, insofar as comparisons can be made, the median term of office has declined below that of 1925. The reasons for this appear to be, first, that these officials

---

[10] See, e.g., the statement by B. C. Forbes, that the "trend is towards younger men" because "the pace is much more strenuous" than earlier, and "more die at a comparatively early age" (*America's Fifty Foremost Business Leaders,* New York: B. C. Forbes, 1948, p. viii).

attained office at a somewhat more advanced age, and second, that retirement plans are beginning to apply to the top officials as well as the other employees. Some corporations, notably Standard Oil of New Jersey, retire chief executives as well as other employees at sixty-five, but that this policy is not yet widespread, as applied to presidents and board chairmen, is clearly indicated by the fact that the average age of retirement is above sixty-five. The average term of office is not markedly different for the different types of business. Consequently, the data have not been broken down by business categories.

TABLE 56

TERMS OF OFFICE OF CORPORATION EXECUTIVES [a]

(*Percentage distribution*)

NUMBER OF YEARS	ENTIRE GROUP		SELECTED GROUP [b]		
	1900	1925	1900	1925	1950
Less than 10	49.7	15.2	75.4	37.6	46.8
10–19	26.0	36.7	17.7	46.1	25.9
20–29	16.8	29.4	5.4	14.5	18.2
30–39	4.4	12.1	0.8	0.9	5.7
40 and over	3.2	6.7	0.8	0.9	3.4
	100.0	100.0	100.0	100.0	100.0
Number of cases	316	330 [c]	130	117	263
Median years of office	10	19	3	12	11

[a] Includes terms as either president or chairman or the two combined. In the few instances where a term was interrupted by some other activity, such as public office, the total years of service as chief executive have been used to determine length of service, deducting years in other activities.

[b] Since the majority of the 1950 group are still in office, only those whose service had terminated prior to January 1, 1955, can be used for this comparison. In order to make the data comparable with earlier periods, only those whose service had terminated prior to January 1, 1905, and January 1, 1930, are included. This tends to include a disproportionately large number of those with short terms of office, but the trends should be indicated by this comparison.

[c] All the 1925 group has been included, although 15 are still in office. The terms of office of these have been taken as of January 1, 1955. All have been in office 30 years or more. Some, however, who have not yet reached the 40-year mark may do so before the end of their term, thus increasing this group at the expense of the 30–39-year group.

The data in Table 56 make it clear that a large proportion of executives do not have the minimum span of office generally regarded as desirable in order to carry through their policies, even though large numbers are allowed to continue in office long after sixty-five. If, in the future, the average age of attaining office should continue to increase as it has in the past, and at the same time an increasing proportion of corporations should retire their top officials at sixty-five, the number getting as much as ten years in office to develop their programs will become a small minority. This raises questions as to how the desired continuity is to be achieved. It is possible that policy determination will become increasingly a group activity, so that frequent changes in the top executives will matter less. Or the trends may be reversed, either through more rapid promotion or the abandonment of early retirement programs.

Comparative figures for total periods of service with the companies these executives eventually headed are given in Table 57. The median years of service for the 1900 group was 15 and for the 1925 group 32. Comparing only those of the 1925 and 1950 executives who had completed their service by January 1, 1930, and January 1, 1955, respectively, the medians were 22 years for the earlier group and 35 years for the later.

A considerable number of executives in each of the three groups have given sixty years or more of service to their companies. The longest service record found in any period among those who have completed their service is that of W. J. Jenks, who started as telegraph operator for the Norfolk and Western Railway in 1886 and rose to the presidency at the age of sixty-six after 50 years of service. At seventy-six he became chairman of the board, and he retired in 1954 at the age of eighty-four, a total service of 68 years. Among those still in office, A. V. Davis, now chairman of the board of Alcoa, has been with his company 66 years. S. H. Kress has been in the retail business continuously for 67 years, although his chain stores are only 58 years old. And George L. Hartford, chairman of the board of the Great Atlantic and Pacific, began as a full-time worker in his father's store in 1880. This gives him 74 years in the same business. Longer working lives have been found. C. W. Nash, for instance, who began work at seven, as noted earlier,[11] had 77 years of work to his credit when he retired shortly before his death in 1948; but his working life covered a great variety of businesses.

[11] See above, p. 88.

It seems probable that in the future the average years of service will increase very little and may even decline. Although the tendency to select the executive from those with long service within the company is, if anything, gaining, this factor will probably be largely offset by the growing requirement of university degrees, which delay the age of beginning work, and by the increasing—although not yet widely accepted—tendency to enforce retirement for top officials as well as for others. The maximum working life between graduation from college and sixty-five is about 45 years. But among the 1950 executives more than one in twenty has already exceeded this span with his company, and the great majority are still serving.

TABLE 57

TOTAL YEARS OF SERVICE WITH CORPORATION

(*Percentage distribution*)

	ENTIRE GROUP		SELECTED GROUP [a]		
NUMBER OF YEARS	*1900*	*1925*	*1900*	*1925*	*1950*
Less than 10	38.7	5.5	62.7	14.7	10.6
10–19	24.3	17.9	18.6	30.2	12.9
20–29	14.1	20.1	10.1	22.4	14.1
30–39	12.1	22.2	3.9	12.1	22.7
40 and over	10.8	34.4	4.7	20.6	39.6
	100.0	100.0	100.0	100.0	100.0
Number of cases	313	329	129	116	255

[a] Those whose services ended before January 1, 1905, 1930, and 1950 respectively.

TERMINATION OF OFFICE

The age of termination of office, like the length of tenure, is available for the entire group only for 1900. However, the record is nearly enough complete for the 1925 group to make comparisons possible, and the same kind of comparison for the three periods can be made for age of termination of office as for the term of office. The median age of termination of office for all executives was 59 for 1900 officials and 70 for the 1925 group. The median age of termination of office for that part of each of the three groups that was out of office before 1905, 1930, and 1955 respectively, was 53, 63, and 67. If there is the same spread between the 1925 and 1950 groups when the 1950 officials finally retire, the median age of retirement for this group will be well over 70. The median ages of termination of office for different kinds of business and for different sizes of corporations are given in Table 58. The variations for most of these are not marked.

The record of reasons for termination of office is necessarily incomplete. The great majority of the 1950 group of executives are still in office, and even for the 1925 group fifteen still held office as of the end of 1954. All the executives included in the 1900 sample are now out of office, although a few of the 1950 group were actually in office in 1900, but were not included in the 1900 sample because their businesses at that time were still small.

TABLE 58

MEDIAN AGE OF TERMINATION OF OFFICE

	ENTIRE GROUP		SELECTED GROUP [a]		
	1900	1925	1900	1925	1950
All corporations	59	70	53	63	67
Railroads	61	69	57	64	66½
Public utilities	58	70	55	57½	68
Industrials	61	70	52	63	66
Largest companies	60	69	57	64	66
Smallest companies	60	70	54	62	65

[a] Those whose service ended before January 1, 1905, 1930, and 1955 respectively.

Since all but a very small number of the 1925 group are now out of office, a comparison between the complete 1900 list and that for 1925 is possible. This is given in Table 59. For 1950 the only comparison that can be made is of the group whose office had terminated by January 1, 1955. These have been compared with the same groups for the two earlier periods, i.e., those out of office by January 1, 1905 and 1930 respectively, in Table 60.

The causes of termination of office are not always clear. Only when individuals die while in office is the reason for termination of office beyond question. For the other groups, the reasons for quitting are likely to be complex and not always frankly stated. The group classified here under retirement are those aged sixty-five and over who appear to have left voluntarily, or because of company retirement

TABLE 59

REASONS FOR TERMINATION OF OFFICE

	NUMBER OF EXECUTIVES		PERCENTAGE OF EXECUTIVES	
	1900	1925	1900	1925
Death	99	157	31.6	51.0
Retirement [a]	58	108	18.5	35.1
Resignation [b]	37	13	11.8	4.2
Other office in company [c]	9	9	2.9	2.9
Change in control [d]	70	16	22.4	5.2
Failure [e]	40	5	12.8	1.6
Total	313	308	100.0	100.0
No information	3	22		

[a] Includes only those who did not go into some other business.
[b] Includes those leaving voluntarily, usually for better position.
[c] Vice chairman of board, chairman of finance committee, vice president, etc.
[d] Includes both those who sold control and those who were appointees of a group which sold out or lost control.
[e] Includes both failures of the company, and failure of the individual to meet the approval of the directors. Failure of the company is responsible for 4.5 percent in 1900 and 1.0 percent in 1925.

TABLE 60

REASONS FOR TERMINATION OF OFFICE OF A
SELECTED GROUP OF EXECUTIVES [a]

(Percentage distribution)

	1900	1925	1950
Death	19.2	38.4	28.7
Retirement	10.8	39.2	46.9
Change in control	36.2	8.0	4.6
Failure	17.7 [b]	.9 [b]	6.1 [b]
Voluntary resignation	14.6	12.5	8.0
Other offices	1.6	.9	5.7
	100.0	100.0	100.0

[a] Those whose services ended before January 1, 1905, 1930, and 1955 respectively.
[b] Failure of the company alone accounts for 6.2 percent in 1900, none in 1925, and 2.0 percent in 1950.

policies, and who have not gone into another business. Voluntary resignations include mostly younger men who have left for other, more attractive, activities. Those who have taken lesser offices in their own companies are usually older men accepting a less demanding position, mostly part-time and advisory. A few, however, have accepted a clear demotion in their own companies. Change in control is sometimes the result of the officer himself selling his holdings in the company, although more often he is the appointee of some other financial interest which has lost control or voluntarily sold out. Failures include both failure of the company, and failure of the officer in question to meet the directors' approval. The actual number of these is probably larger than the figures in Tables 59 and 60 indicate, since financial difficulties often result in change in control or in consolidation with more successful concerns rather than in winding up the business. And where the individual himself is unsuccessful, he may appear on the public record as retiring or resigning voluntarily to take another position. It is exceptional for an open split to occur.

The comparatively small proportion of the 1900 executives, as compared with the later groups, who retired or died in office reflects the revolutionary changes in business organization and control that were taking place in this period. Under the more settled conditions of the nineteen-twenties the great majority of officers either retired or died in office. The relative proportions of those dying and retiring shift somewhat for the 1950 group, nearly half of those out of office to date having retired. This change is to be expected, as a combined result of the increase in automatic retirement practices and the increase in average length of life. Death and retirement combined account for about the same proportion of cases in each of the two later periods.

There has been some recurrence in the past year or so in fights for control of even the very large companies, and recurrence, also, in combinations. The shifts in control in the New York Central, the New York, New Haven and Hartford, and the Central of Georgia railways are instances of the first, and the combinations among the second-rank automobile companies are instances of the second. Other cases, including several not yet settled, could be cited. But they do not bulk large enough to have much influence on the proportions of those out of office for these reasons.

CHAPTER NINE

INCENTIVES FOR HOLDING
EXECUTIVE OFFICE

The opportunities for personal power and for creative work are, if not limitless, certainly very great. In this respect, non-financial rewards may provide a more powerful stimulus than monetary compensation to the business executive in the large corporation.

R. A. GORDON

IN earlier chapters the question has been raised whether the process of selecting chief executives insures discovery of the best-qualified men. But the choice of those best qualified for office is not the only problem: those chosen must also be eager to accept. Consequently, it is essential that the position be more attractive than alternative opportunities.

The most important factors in attracting the best talent are, probably: (1) that the position itself should prove interesting and challenging; (2) that remuneration should be adequate; (3) that the position should offer a reasonable degree of security; and (4) that it should carry with it prestige.

There seems to be almost complete agreement as to the attractiveness of the work itself. The nature of the job is changing. With the increasing age and size of the corporation there is less need for the dictator and more need for individuals who know how to take advice and to gain their ends by persuasion. But while this requires a different type of leader from those who were organizing new, and for the most part smaller, businesses, it does not mean that it is more difficult to induce able men to accept the job. The job itself is not an easy one. The heavy responsibilities resting on the top executive

The quotation at the head of this chapter is taken from R. A. Gordon, *Business Leadership in the Large Corporation*, Washington: Brookings, 1945, p. 314.

officers are recognized. However, although there is an occasional defection from the ranks,[1] there is every indication that the majority of executives work overtime—not because it is necessary in order to keep the job but because they are absorbed in their work. Complaints about long hours and short vacations come from their wives and their subordinates rather than from the men themselves. These assertions are widely accepted, but they have been documented recently by a study of 111 top executives in California, with salaries of $35,000 or more, summarized in *Time*.[2] This study found that the majority worked overtime—from 67 to 112 hours a week; and that these, but not their wives, were happier than the minority who worked normal or less than normal hours.

Remuneration, too, appears to be attractive. A good deal of complaint is found—particularly in communications to stockholders—about the small proportion of the salary that is left after taxes. But this discussion appears to be of a defensive nature, directed to stockholders, who have frequently questioned the high remuneration of top officials. The real test, of course, is how remuneration for these jobs compares with remuneration for other important positions.

No salary data are available for the two earlier periods, but they are available for the 1950 group of executives, except for a few recent appointees and for some in closely held corporations. Remuneration is not limited to salaries. Most of the large corporations have private pension plans that make liberal provision for the top executives. Also, there has been a recurrence in recent years of bonus payments, usually called "incentive compensation payments," since the term "bonus" appears to have fallen into disrepute. And many corporations offer their executives stock options as an extra inducement. Finally, the expense account often provides luxuries that the salary alone would hardly justify.

The expense accounts, like the pension systems, have expanded with high taxes. Many companies tolerate generous allowances in the belief that it makes for satisfied officers and in recognition of the

---

[1] See, e.g., T. K. Quinn, *Giant Business*, New York: Exposition Press, 1953, p. 159.
[2] Study by A. S. Talbott reported in *Time*, November 10, 1952, p. 109. See also William H. Whyte, Jr., "How Hard Do Executives Work?" *Fortune*, XLIX, No. 1 (January, 1954), 108ff.

fact that a large part of the cost would otherwise go for taxes. Allowable expenses frequently include club memberships, entertainment in the home, and travel expenses for wives of high executives, especially if the wife's presence "is considered to be a definite business asset," [3] and, of course, first-class hotel and travel accommodations. Whyte's comment, that "the expense account has become a way of life," indicates its importance.[4] The tendency for the big corporation to absorb the social life of its executives has disadvantages for the executives and their families, but it provides substantial material gains.

The remuneration of the 1950 group, as far as it is reported in the notices of annual meetings, is given in Table 61. The great majority of the executives—85 percent—received remuneration in excess of $50,000, even though the group includes several chairmen whose positions were part time or honorary, and who received no regular salary. Moreover, this figure does not cover all forms of remuneration. The expense account, the value of stock options, and in some cases the corporation's contribution to the pension fund are not included.[5]

The salaries paid by the industrial companies are much higher on the average than those paid by the railroads and public utilities, in spite of the fact that the railroads and public utilities are larger, on the average, in terms of assets. However, a comparison of salaries paid by the corporations classified by size shows that the compensation of the officials of the larger companies runs somewhat higher than that of officials of the smaller companies, although the difference is not as marked as the difference in size might lead one to expect. There is very little difference between the earlier and later appointees, indicating that there is very little increase for long service.

The higher proportion of payments under $50,000 for chairmen

[3] National Industrial Conference Board, "Executive Expense Accounts," *Studies in Business Policy*, No. 67 (1954), p. 12.

[4] William H. Whyte, Jr., *Is Anybody Listening?* New York: Simon and Schuster, 1952, p. 171.

[5] Stock options are becoming an increasingly important factor in executive remuneration. See, e.g., Perrin Stryker, "Do Stock Options Pay?" in *Fortune*, L, No. 6 (December, 1954), 118.

TABLE 61

REMUNERATION OF EXECUTIVES, 1950 [a]

(Percentage distribution)

BY TYPE OF COMPANY

Remuneration	Railroad	Public Utility	Industrial	All Types
$50,000 or Less	45.4	39.6	15.1	23.4
$51,000–$100,000	43.2	48.6	34.9	38.5
$101,000–$200,000	11.4	10.4	41.9	32.2
Over $200,000	. . .	1.4	8.1	5.9
	100.0	100.0	100.0	100.0

BY SIZE OF COMPANY

(Assets in millions of dollars)

	100 or Less	101–200	201–500	Over 500
$50,000 or Less	29.0	27.8	20.9	11.1
$51,000–$100,000	41.4	38.9	35.3	37.8
$101,000–$200,000	28.6	30.5	33.7	38.5
Over $200,000	1.0	2.8	10.2	12.6
	100.0	100.0	100.0	100.0

BY OFFICE AND TIME OF APPOINTMENT

	Presidents	Chairmen	Earlier Appointees	Later Appointees
$50,000 or Less	16.1	35.7	24.3	22.7
$51,000–$100,000	43.1	30.7	36.5	40.1
$101,000–$200,000	34.8	27.8	31.9	32.5
Over $200,000	5.9	5.8	7.3	4.7
	100.0	100.0	100.0	100.0

[a] Includes salaries, incentive compensation, and other remuneration as reported in notices of annual meetings. Data are for 748 of the 882 executives in the 1950 group.

than for presidents is due to the fact that the chairmen include a number of part-time or partially retired individuals, whereas the presidents do not. However, for the majority of chairmen who are full-time employees there is no important difference in compensation between chairmen and presidents. Some companies pay the chairman more than the president, and some pay him the same amount. If he is on full time and has previously been president, he is not likely to be paid less, even when the president holds the position of chief executive. Reduction of salary with the shift from president to chairman is rare.

Incentive compensation is largely responsible for the very high remuneration of a few. Among the 44 executives receiving more than $200,000, approximately half obtained incentive compensation payments in excess of $50,000, and eleven obtained incentive compensation payments that exceeded their salaries. All five of those whose remuneration exceeded $400,000 obtained the larger part of their compensation in this way. Board chairmen are quite regularly included in incentive compensation schemes—another indication of the increasingly active nature of this office. In the nineteen-twenties and thirties the chairmen did not usually participate in bonus payments.[6]

No comparable data on remuneration are available for the earlier groups of executives. There is evidence, however, that the current group has a different standard of living than the 1900 group, and perhaps a more modest one. The palaces are gone, and with them most of the racing stables and art collections. The homes of today's executives are very modest affairs compared with the Newport mansions. And yachts, if they exist at all, are smaller and simpler.[7] On the other hand, there are the executive planes; and some business conventions, and the combined business and pleasure trips, all paid for by the company, take on the aspect of a luxurious holiday. It is more likely to be the lesser executives than the top brass that regard these as an important perquisite of the job, although the generosity of the company in regard to expense accounts is greater with high officials than with lesser ones.

For the 1925 executives, some financial data are available in the form of the tax returns made public for 1923 and 1924 incomes. Among those listed in the *New York Times*,[8] which is by no means a complete listing, are 111 (or one out of every three officers of the 1925 group) whose taxes indicate incomes in excess of $75,000. Of

[6] R. A. Gordon, *Business Leadership in the Large Corporation*, Washington: Brookings, 1945, p. 291.

[7] The October, 1951, issue of *Fortune* contains an interesting collection of photographs of the homes and yachts of executives, present and earlier, and also of company planes.

[8] October 24 to November 14, 1924, and September 2 to 11, 1925.

these, 68 represent incomes between $100,000 and $500,000, 20 represent incomes in excess of $500,000. These taxes were paid on *all* income, of course, and not just on income received from the corporations for services; but in most instances such information as has been found from other sources indicates that the larger part of the income came from the corporation, whether as salary, bonus, or dividends. It is hardly necessary to add that such incomes placed the executives among the élite. The tax returns for 1923 and 1924 indicate that only about one family in 10,000 had an income in excess of $100,-000, as compared with better than one in four for the executives. There is other evidence that compensation was adequate in this period. In fact, it was at this time that the stockholders of Bethlehem Steel and other corporations began to criticize the bonus as an undue reward to their top executives.

Although statistical data for the 1900 executives are not available, there are other indications that salaries and bonuses were of less importance for a large proportion of this group than return on their own investments in the corporations, or profits from financial manipulation. Some "bought" the presidency in the stock market and gave it up when they were successful in selling their holdings at a profit, or overreached their resources and failed. Some organized new companies with the expectation of immediate profit from the sale of security flotations. And some were satisfied to wait for dividends as the corporation prospered. Many, of course, were salaried executives like the great majority of the 1950 group. This was particularly true of the railroad presidents. But there were enough of the financiers to overshadow the others in publicity and perhaps even in numbers.[9]

By 1925 the large corporations were for the most part at least a generation old. This increased the number of inheritors, as compared with the earlier period, and it also provided opportunity for new executives to come up within the corporation through their own merit and efforts. Consequently, the proportion of executives with long experience within the corporation increased greatly. Very few regarded the office as a means for a quick profit. If their holdings were large, they were also fairly permanent. Even the organizers and

[9] Note that 54.5 percent of this group attained office either through investment, inheritance or participating in the organization of the company. See above, p. 102.

investors tended to hold office for long periods. And the proportion of those working up within the corporation, and largely dependent on their salaries, had doubled as compared with the 1900 group. They were still, however, a wealthy group, and a fairly powerful one. The small stockholders had not yet begun to insist on the kind of accounting that they expect today. And the government, too, was less demanding then than now. Moreover, times were prosperous and the job offered security. The pension systems provided for to-day's executives did not exist, but more than half of the top officials died in office, and only 7 percent left because of changes in control or failure due either to bankruptcy of the company or to their own ejection by dissatisfied boards of directors.

The 1950 executives are characteristically salaried administrators. They have greater security than most groups of employees. They are rarely dismissed; the accepted age of retirement is older than for ordinary employees; and the pension plans are generous and almost universal. Most of them, however, are dependent on their salaries and other forms of compensation rather than on investments.

The adequacy of this compensation, in most instances, is indicated by the fact that no other group of individuals can be found who are paid more. Occasionally a film or television star receives a salary equal to the best of these, but the number of years of high earnings for such individuals are few compared with the executives, even though they come earlier in life. High government positions do not command equivalent compensation. The president of the United States presumably holds the top position in this country, but his salary is exceeded by seventy members of this group of executives.[10]

There has been more question as to whether the executives are overpaid than as to whether they are underpaid, and it is sometimes suggested that since they are members of the board of directors they are in a position to set their own salaries. It is, of course, customary to appoint only outsiders on the board to the salary committees, but the committees are usually appointed by the recipients of the salaries,

[10] The President's salary is $150,000, including a $50,000 taxable expense account. In addition, of course, some of his living expenses are covered from other sources. Owing to the lack of comparative data on the amount of the expense accounts and the extent to which they contribute to individual planes of living, exact comparisons are not possible.

and there are not always outsiders on the board to take on this task.

In view of this criticism, a comparison has been made of the compensation of officials in companies where the board is made up wholly or predominantly of officials and in companies where outsiders make up the majority of the board. The results, given in Table 62, indicate that the inside boards are less generous with their chiefs than the outside boards. Since the number of cases is comparatively small, this difference may be accidental, but it is clear, at least, that the inside boards are not more generous than the outside boards. This, too, indicates that compensation is satisfactory.

But if remuneration is, on the whole, satisfactory, it is not closely related to the apparent demands of the position. The tendency to provide higher remuneration in the larger corporations is a reasonable one, since the top positions in the larger corporations presumably carry with them greater responsibilities and the need for greater talent than in the case of the smaller ones. But the tendency is not as marked as might be expected in view of the great differences in the size of the corporations themselves. The median salary for the executives of the largest group of corporations, those with assets in excess of $500,000,000, is about one-third more than that for the smallest

TABLE 62

COMPARISON OF REMUNERATION OF EXECUTIVES AUTHORIZED BY
INSIDE AND OUTSIDE BOARDS OF DIRECTORS, 1952

Percentage of Inside Members on Board	Number of Companies	Number of Executives	Median Salary
100	13	32	$100,000
50–99	37	90	$110,000
Less than 50	37	87	$125,000

group, those with assets below $100,000,000. Moreover, the medians do not reveal the many variations from the norm. Seven executives among the corporations with assets below $100,000,000 received a larger remuneration than the president of American Telephone and Telegraph, which has assets in excess of $10,000,000,000—more than one hundred times the size of the smaller corporations noted. And twenty-nine executives among the smallest group of corporations received higher remuneration than the president of the largest railroad. There appears to be no good reason why industrials should, on the average, pay higher sums to their executives than the railroads and public utilities except, of course, that the latter groups are subject to stricter government regulation than the industrials.

This raises the question: Do the higher salaries attract greater talent? If so, the railroads and public utilities are, perhaps, not paying enough. It is occasionally stated that railroad executives as a group have been less able than industrial executives [11] and that the lower compensation may be responsible in part.

There is also the question: Do incentive compensation payments stimulate greater effort? This claim was advanced in support of the bonus payments of the nineteen twenties, and it is being repeated today. But when the depression of the thirties reduced profits or eliminated them altogether, the executives were not held responsible for the decline. On the contrary, salaries were in many instances increased to cover some of the losses from the shrinking bonus payments. Gordon records a 16-percent increase in executive salaries between 1929 and 1931 for thirty-six companies paying bonuses in 1929. The total compensation, of course, declined.[12] All of the evidence that has been found supports Gordon's contention [13] that pride in the corporation and in a job well done are the strongest motivating forces. This is the normal outcome of the professionalization of the job.

And finally there is the question: What are the tests of efficiency? David C. Coyle, for instance, challenges the worth of Gary to the United States Steel Corporation, noting that he first lost Schwab to Bethlehem Steel and then refused Henry Gray's invention of wide-flanged beams, which Bethlehem, under Schwab, accepted and from which it made a handsome profit.[14] On the other hand, Gary may well have been worth what he was paid if his great achievement, as a *New York Times* editorial states, was to keep the United States Steel Corporation free from antitrust prosecution.[15] Gary's salary was re-

[11] See, e.g., Gordon, *Business Leadership*, p. 276.
[12] *Ibid.*, p. 288. [13] *Ibid.*, pp. 308–10.
[14] *New York Times Magazine*, January 30, 1949, pp. 38–39.
[15] *New York Times*, August 16, 1927, p. 24.

puted to have been $100,000 or more at the time of his death.[16] His 1924 income tax indicated a total income of between $500,000 and $1,000,000. Only five other executives were found in the 1925 group whose taxes were reported as being higher.

To summarize, it is clear that compensation of top executives bears some relation to the magnitude of the task, but deviations from the average are many and erratic. There is a large element of chance in the amount of the rewards of office. The financial compensation offered for some executive positions, particularly among the railroads, may be inadequate to attract the talent needed, but for most positions it appears to be ample. Certainly the financial rewards are far larger, and accompanied by greater security, than the salaries of top government jobs that, judged by the funds handled alone, are comparable in magnitude.

The third factor that makes the job of the corporation executive attractive is the unusual degree of security it offers. This statement is based on two types of evidence. The first lies in the reasons for termination of office. Eighty-six percent of the 1925 group either retired at the age of 65 or later, or died in office. The median age of quitting was 70. Of the remaining 14 percent, about half appear to have quit voluntarily. Indications are that the position offers comparable security for the present group. The median age of termination of office, for those already out, is 67. For the whole group it will undoubtedly be substantially higher. Even when retirement at 65 or earlier is required for lesser employees, the top executives are often exempted. A very small proportion, as in the case of the 1925 executives, has been forced out of office, and some of those who have left of their own free will have been welcomed back when they tired of other activities. Donald B. Lourie, president of Quaker Oats, for instance, resigned to take the position of Under Secretary of State early in 1953. A little over a year later he returned to Quaker Oats and was reelected president, his successor being given a vice chairmanship. And Paul G. Hoffman resigned the presidency of Studebaker in 1948 to become ECA administrator and returned to Studebaker in 1953 as board chairman.

[16] *Ibid.*, p. 3.

The other factor—a comparatively new one—that contributes to security is the rapid growth in private pension plans. These have been adopted partly to make it easier to enforce retirement sometime between sixty-five and seventy. But they have been stimulated, also, by the favorable tax treatment given this form of compensation as compared with salaries, and one of their functions is to reduce turnover.

The final consideration in making these positions attractive is the degree of prestige that they command. This is not a factor that can be measured statistically, but it is clearly high, even though there are some indications that in this respect the 1950 executives may have lost a little ground as compared with the 1900 executives. One test of this is publicity. The position has lost much of its news value. These men are not creating new empires such as those of Rockefeller, Carnegie, Morgan, and the railroad builders of the second half of the nineteenth century. Nor are they often engaged in battles for financial control, although the recent instances of the fights for control of the New Haven railroad, the New York Central, and Montgomery Ward testify to the newsworthiness of this kind of activity. They are carrying on well-organized concerns in the accepted tradition. They rarely seek publicity. And the willingness of those who have been invited to take high government office to accept, even at considerable financial sacrifice, is evidenced by the response to President Eisenhower's invitations. Two of the 1950 executives gave up important posts to join the Cabinet, and two more accepted offices just below Cabinet rank. Nor is this unique. All recent administrations have had one or two prominent bankers or corporation executives in their Cabinets. Although the total number of cases is small, this appears to be because the opportunities are few. The prestige of the corporation executive, great as it is, apparently cannot compete with the prestige of cabinet office. And the executives are prepared to make substantial financial sacrifices to gain this prestige. This does not mean that the position of chief executive of a large business corporation is in any way lacking in prestige; only that here, and here alone, it is possible for important government offices to compete.

CHAPTER TEN

QUALIFICATIONS FOR THE SUCCESSFUL EXECUTIVE

Industrial experts, engineers, chemists, mineralogists, technicians of all kinds, have been drifting into more responsible positions in the industrial system and have been growing up and multiplying within the system, because the system will no longer work at all without them.

THORSTEIN VEBLEN

THE foregoing discussion indicates that there is little or no problem of inducing individuals with the desired qualifications to accept the top executive positions. The other question is whether the present practices in appointing top executives are those best designed to find the ablest individuals. Here the evidence is inconclusive.

There has been a very active search in recent years for talented young men to come in at the bottom—college graduates ready to start their business or professional careers. The search sometimes goes higher. A few corporations have raided university faculties for talent. But even at this point what the companies are looking for is promising scientists, engineers, lawyers, or accountants. They are not looking for future presidents and board chairmen, or even primarily for good administrators at a lower level. Yet in the end it will be from this group that the future president or board chairman will most frequently come. Two out of three of the top executives appointed in the period 1944 to 1953 inclusive had been with their companies more than ten years before assuming the top position. And one out of every four (25.4 percent) of the appointees of the last ten years has had no experience outside his own company. They are successful lawyers, engineers, and accountants who have risen within the com-

The quotation at the head of this chapter is taken from Thorstein Veblen, *The Engineers and the Price System*, New York: Huebsch, 1921, p. 44.

pany thanks to the qualities that made them successful in their professions. But these are not necessarily the qualities that make for successful top administrators. Even granting that they have been selected from among their fellows because they have shown more talent for administration than the others, it does not follow that a wider search for talent might not reveal better administrators.

The number that is chosen from outside is substantial. Indeed, it increased among the recent 1950 appointees as compared with the earlier ones. But the increase was at the expense of inheritors and organizers. And the proportion that worked up within the company increased more than the proportion brought in from outside jobs.

This does not mean, of course, that the quality of management is declining. There is a fairly good chance that the executive who has worked up within the company as a result of his own ability and effort is better qualified than are the heirs. And as the corporations increase in size, they have more and more talent to select from. But many express doubts as to the soundness of the inside training. The larger the corporation, the more specialized its vice presidents are likely to be. And the scientists and lawyers are trained to weigh all the evidence carefully and present all sides of the problem, whereas the top executive has to make decisions, often before all the evidence is in. Moreover, the engineers and the scientists are trained to deal with things, whereas top management, since it is more and more a cooperative job, increasingly demands talent for dealing with people. The experts on personal relations, who seem to have one of the more important qualifications for the top job, are rarely represented. Only one executive has been found who clearly reached the top through the personnel department, although there are a number who have had some experience in personnel departments, and almost every vice president must have been in charge of a large staff of employees and had ample opportunity to demonstrate his ability to deal with people.

The nature of the executive job, and the qualifications which should be sought when candidates for the job are under consideration, are indicated by the following quotations from experienced executives and other authorities. According to *Fortune,* President

Stolk of American Can says, "My job is mostly talking with people." [1] And J. E. Janney quotes the President of Dixie Cup as saying that almost all of his activities involve human relations.[2] Janney also quotes the President of Pitney Bowes, Inc., as saying that 70 percent of his time goes to problems of human relations.[3] And Greenewalt says; "An executive is good when he can make a smoothly functioning team out of people with the many different skills required in the operation of a modern business.[4]

Wald and Doty report that the majority of thirty-three executives interviewed "stated that skill in human relations was most important in their own advancement. Important qualities in this connection were ability to get along with people, social poise, consideration of others, and tact in personal dealings." [5] And James W. Simpson writes:

Management seems to be the one field where a man expects to advance, not necessarily because he is capable of managing, but because he has previously been a success in a specialists' job. This is hit-and-miss selection and it doesn't always work out well. The engineer doesn't always make a good manager; nor does the sales manager, the production manager, or anyone else, unless he has the qualifications and training required of a "management generalist." . . . In what should a specialist be trained in order to become a generalist? Ability in human relations transcends all else.[6]

Janney's summary of the duties of the top executive is: (1) to get work done by others; (2) to take responsibility for others; and (3) to spend more time and effort on human relations and less on technical relations.[7] Finally, Donald K. David's "ideal business man" would

[1] *Fortune*, XLVI, No. 4 (October, 1952), p. 148.
[2] "Company Presidents Look at Themselves," *Harvard Business Review*, XXX, No. 3 (May–June, 1952), 59.
[3] *Ibid.*
[4] C. H. Greenewalt, "We're Going to Need More Executives," Speech before Executives' Club of Chicago, May 1, 1953.
[5] R. M. Wald and R. A. Doty, "The Top Executives—A Firsthand Profile," *Harvard Business Review*, XXXII, No. 4 (July–August, 1954), 50.
[6] *The Clarkson Letter*, January, 1954.
[7] Janney, "Company Presidents Look at Themselves," *Harvard Business Review*, XXX, No. 3 (May–June, 1952), 59.

(1) have the ability to work effectively with people; (2) have the ability to make decisions; (3) instinctively accept responsibility; (4) understand the basic forces at work in our society and recognize the weaknesses and deficiencies in our system; and (5) have a clear understanding of his objectives, lying mainly in the area of furnishing both material and other human satisfactions.[8]

These examples are a few of the many that have been found pointing to the consensus that the top executive needs broader training than the specialists are apt to get, and that the primary job of the executive is to deal with people, to persuade them to give their own best efforts, and to cooperate with others toward the common end. Not all the comments found are as emphatic about this as those quoted, but none has been found that contradicts this point of view.

This suggests that the best training for the top executive position in the big corporation would be a comparable position in a smaller corporation where his success has already been demonstrated. And this, of course, is the history of some executives. Supplee of Atlantic Refinery was taken from a milk company, and Nance of Packard was president of Hotpoint, to cite specific cases. Most of the 18 percent of the 1950 executives that were chosen for success in other companies could meet this test, although some had positions of lesser responsibility. Also, some of the 4 percent classified as "other" were presidents of independent companies later consolidated with the one they now head, and presumably had demonstrated ability, although they were not necessarily competing with a large number of other potential candidates. But none of the increasing group of executives that has worked up within the company has had the responsibility of a top position except for a scattering few that have headed subsidiaries without important interference from the parent company.

Many companies are aware of the discrepancy between the standards set by the authorities for the chief executive position and the actual training and experience of the second-ranking officers from whom the future executives will probably be chosen. Their answer

[8] Speech quoted in *New York Herald Tribune,* June 10, 1949, p. 9.

to the problem is, however, not to increase the search outside of the company for top level men but to make more effort to train their own men for the top job. This is done in various ways. Sometimes a likely top administrator is groomed for the job by being made assistant to the president, with perhaps a final stint as executive vice president. Sometimes a group of promising candidates are given special training. This is likely to include both rotation of job within the company, to remove the curse of specialization, and perhaps a short course given by some recognized graduate school of business, to give the individuals concerned some perspective on their own company. Standard Oil of New Jersey, e.g., has been operating an "executive development program" for about ten years. This has been described in a recent speech by one of their directors.[9] He emphasized both the importance of rotation on the job and off-the-job training in advanced management courses. However, he stated that most of the training can be acquired within the company, and while he noted that some of their trainees have been pulled off to other companies, he did not suggest that Standard Oil of New Jersey itself might seek talent elsewhere.

Standard Oil of New Jersey is one of the most self-sufficient of the big corporations, with a completely inside board, most of the members of which have worked up within the company. Only one of the 1953 group, a banker by training, had had long experience in other fields. All had been with the company at least nine years, and half had been with the company more than thirty years before becoming directors. The recently retired board chairman, Abrams, started with the company in 1912. The present chairman, Holman, was president of Humble Oil before becoming president of the parent company, and Rathbone was president of Esso before becoming president of Standard. This kind of experience should have given them adequate opportunity to demonstrate their ability to guide the parent company.

No criticism has been found of the management of Standard Oil of New Jersey. On the contrary, it appears to be regarded as among the more progressive and best-managed of the big companies. Con-

[9] John R. Suman. Reprinted in a pamphlet, "Growing a Good Executive Crop," 1954.

trolling an empire, as it does, with the presidencies of subsidiaries, the assets of which exceed half a billion dollars, in which to train the future presidents of the parent company, it is in a position which few even of the largest companies can rival for the training of its own future top executives. Nor do most companies have as many second-rank executives from which to select their talent. Mr. Suman mentions, at one point, that more than four hundred members of their group have taken advanced-management training courses at one or another of the leading schools of business administration. In other words, selection from within such an empire is a very different thing from selection within a corporation with no large subsidiaries.

There is another factor, also, that is rarely mentioned but undoubtedly plays an important part in the tendency to select from within. This is the factor of morale. A company that is in the habit of selecting its top officials from within its own executive group is probably in a position to hold its ablest men more effectively than one which regularly seeks outside talent.

The fact remains, however, that when policies are clearly stated, the preference appears to be for choosing executives with a wide outside experience. And the actual explanation for so much selection from within is probably not that this is, in fact, where the best talent and training lie, but that there is a tendency to prefer the familiar to the unfamiliar. The capacities and limitations of the inside group are better known. The risks are correspondingly less. Moreover, personal preferences that have no rational basis must, in the end, influence choices in many cases.

In conclusion, it appears that most of those who have studied the problem would favor a wider search for talent than now in fact takes place. Particularly, they would favor more frequent bidding for successful heads of smaller corporations. They deplore both specialization and the lack of outside experience. They place great emphasis on success in human relations. And they would prefer appointments of younger men.

An attempt has been made to test the validity of these judgments by comparing the training and experience of the executives of fast-growing and static companies, using the change in assets between 1924 and 1949 as the test of growth.[10] The results of this comparison appear to support the conclusions of the authorities on administration, if it can be assumed that the fast-growing companies have more efficient administration than the static ones.

In view of the fact that the change in corporate assets took place over a twenty-five-year period and many of the 1950 corporation officials had been appointed too late in this period to be credited with any responsibility for growth or failure to grow, all officials who had been in office less than three years during this period were eliminated for this comparison, and earlier officers who had held office for at least three years at some time in this twenty-five-year period were added. This resulted in a group of 124 officials for the rapidly growing corporations, 31 of whom had not been included among the 1950 officials, and 144 officials for the static corporations, 48 of whom had not been included among the 1950 officials.

With respect to education, while a slightly larger proportion of the officers of the fast-growing companies than of the static companies graduated from college (50.7 percent as compared with 47.5 percent), a substantially smaller proportion had graduate training (9.3 percent as compared with 15.5 percent). A large part of this difference is due to advanced degrees in law, there being just twice as many among the officials of the static companies as among the officials of the fast-growing companies. Advanced degrees in engineering also appear with greater frequency among the officials of the static corporations than among those of the fast-growing corporations, although the difference is not as marked as in the case of the law degrees.[11]

There is also an important age differential. The median age of appointment was 46 for the officers of the fast-growing companies and 51 for the officers of the static companies. Also, while the average

[10] See p. 81 for exact definition of fast-growing and static companies.

[11] Differences in the percentages quoted in this paragraph and those found in Table 33, p. 82, are due to the fact that the officers included in Table 33 are those holding office in these companies as of 1948 to 1953, whereas the above figures are for such officers as held the top position for three years or more between 1925 and 1950. Both comparisons show much the same differences in formal education between the officers of the fast-growing and static corporations.

term of office was three years longer for the officers of the fast-growing companies than of the static companies, they were two years younger, on the average, when they retired. Thus these fast-growing companies have achieved a longer term of office for their top officials and have still retired them earlier. They have not demanded as long a period of service with the corporation (9 years on the average as compared with 17) before promoting these officials to the top position. Also, they have taken a larger proportion of their chief executives from outside (17.1 percent as compared with 8.9 percent). This is in spite of the fact that, being a little younger, these fast-growing companies have a larger proportion of their organizers still in office. The static companies, on the other hand, have more officers who represent the investors (12.5 percent as compared with 8.5 percent). The percentage of officers that worked up within the company is 31.6 for the fast-growing companies and 45.9 for the static companies.

These data are not, of course, conclusive evidence as to the importance of drawing talent from outside, the importance of avoiding specialized education, and the importance of bringing in younger executives. The number of cases is too small, and the rate of increase of assets is not, alone, a completely satisfactory measure of success. And finally, there are differences in the nature of the two groups of corporations that must be taken into account.

The two outstanding differences in the nature of the companies are in their average age and in the nature of their businesses. With regard to the kind of business, the fast-growing companies include more oil companies than the static, and the static include more steel companies than the fast-growing. The meatpackers are well represented in the static group with no representation in the fast-growing group, and the aircraft companies are found only in the fast-growing group. However, both groups are well distributed over the entire industrial field.

With regard to age, the fast-growing companies are, on the average, a little younger, and six were still in the hands of their organizers, whereas this was not true for any of the static group. In order to eliminate this difference, a second tabulation was made, excluding the officers of the ten newest of the fast-growing companies.

The median age of the remaining companies was the same as that of the static companies, and the newest company in each group was established in 1918 for the fast-growing group and in 1916 for the static group. This retabulation showed no marked differences between the executives of the younger and older corporations in the fast-growing group. Such small differences as appeared accentuated rather than reduced the contrast between the officers of the fast-growing and the static companies. In short, the limited evidence that this study offers supports the judgments of the authorities quoted earlier as to the qualifications for the successful executive.

CHAPTER ELEVEN

THE PROFESSION OF
BUSINESS
ADMINISTRATION

Many look upon the advance of technology as reason to assume the engineers and technical people will take over at the top. But the reverse is probably more likely to occur. Technicians there will have to be, but the top managers will have to know less about technology—depending on the specialists to provide them with correct information. . . . It may even be difficult to train such men in big companies. Some look ahead to the day when top management will be culled from the ranks of small businesses. . . . But however the management man of the future is trained he will be a specialist in his own right.

A BUSINESS EXECUTIVE

IN summarizing the findings of this study it should be emphasized that the data cover practically all the chief executives of the large corporations in the railroad, public utility, and industrial fields. They cannot be assumed to be representative, however, of either the large financial corporations or the small corporations in the fields included. Also, it cannot be assumed that the trends indicated for the period studied will continue for the indefinite future. They are related to changes in the economy and in government regulations that are partly accidental and may easily shift their course. In fact, it is quite probable, as indicated earlier in this study, that some of these trends will be arrested or even reversed in another generation. But for the limited area and period covered, these data reflect the actual changes in training and experience of the chief executives of our

The quotation at the head of this chapter is taken from *Business Week*, August 15, 1953, p. 53.

corporations and the variations in their training and experience at any one period.

The beginning of the twentieth century was a period of financial manipulation. Large combinations were being formed from going concerns, and many new and large projects were launched for immediate return rather than long-run growth. In consequence, the characteristic head of the big corporation was a "money maker." Approximately half of the 1900 executives of this study had obtained executive office either through participation in the organization of the corporation or through later purchase of financial control. This group includes executives who had founded, almost single-handed, a new and enduring enterprise, but in large part it was made up of bankers and the agents of bankers who had launched new combinations or bought control of those organized by others for the purpose of making a quick profit on the sale of securities or of promoters who were operating on perilously narrow margins and engaging in questionable financial practices—gambling on the chance of unloading their watered stock before the inevitable crash.

Today, in the middle of the twentieth century, the big combinations have come of age. They are no longer in the hands of the founders or even the heirs of their founders. With rare exceptions they are too large to be controlled by a single family fortune. Ownership is widely dispersed, and those in control are hired men. They have been selected either for their success as administrators in other companies or—more frequently—from among the corporation's own officers. They are professional administrators.

Along with this dispersion of ownership has come a distribution of authority. The job has grown with the size of the company, and no investor with scattered interests can direct one of these giants successfully through some agent even if he has sufficient capital to give him legal control. Thus the professional administrator is rarely a banker's or investor's agent. Nor is he often a dictator in his own right. Rather, there are likely to be two professional administrators serving in top executive posts—the president and the board chairman. And while one of these will probably be designated "chief executive officer" there is a real division of power. In addition, the executive vice president and the finance chairman may be endowed with important powers. And the final authority—the board of directors—is more often than not made up in substantial part of these and other officers. Whether they exercise the power or not, the vice presidents are often in the position of being able to outvote the chief executives.

This makes the job of chief executive a very different one from that of either the founders or the financiers. He takes over a well-organized concern. He will be considered successful if he holds the organization together and makes moderate profits. It is important to persuade those under him to work together effectively. It is not necessary—nor perhaps even wise—to take great risks.

There is still a place for innovators and risk takers. But innovation is likely to take the form of adding a new activity to a well-established business, and the risk is a limited one at best. New ventures may be financed from surplus profits, and if they result in loss, the business as a whole can absorb it. In any event, the chief executives share the responsibility, as well as the power, with others.

Some of the obvious reasons for these developments are, first, the success of the big combinations formed at the beginning of the century. Some failed, but many survived and prospered. Consequently, today's big corporations are bigger—and also older. Most of the founders are dead, and most of the heirs have lost control. Ownership, as noted above, is widely dispersed. The small stockholder is in the ascendancy, partly because more people have more money to invest, and partly because, with the inadequacy of the larger fortunes, the small investor receives more encouragement and more protection than he did in the earlier period.

A second change is in the growth of government control. This has curbed the more questionable forms of financial manipulation, limited the control of those at the top, and given the big corporation some of the attributes of a public rather than a private organization.

Along with this, and closely related to it, has come a shift in the attitude of the general public toward big business. There is less suspicion of the large corporation than formerly. But at the same time big business is expected to operate in the public interest. The small stockholder has equal claims with the large to being kept informed of the affairs of the corporation and to receive his share of the profits. And profits must be "reasonable." The public interest extends to the employee, the customer, and even to those with no direct dealings with the corporation. As long ago as the nineteen-twenties Owen Young placed the interest of the employees first, the customers second, and the stockholders third in the concern of management. But he did not include the general public.[1] Today, the community in which the corporation operates expects it to contribute to the community chest and expects its officers to take an active part in community affairs. And it has national obligations—to contribute to institutions of higher learning, perhaps, or to release its officers for government service in times of crisis.

The business executives themselves for the most part appear to accept these obligations in good faith. They sometimes even promote them. Many have a genuine sense of public responsibility, although some, doubtless, submit with such grace as they can muster because they see the way the wind is blowing. In any event, the standard of business ethics has risen as becomes a gradually emerging new profession. It is not that the standards of businessmen at the turn of the century were universally low. J. P. Morgan certainly had high standards. But his standards were his own; they were not derived from a code established by his social group. And many business practices that would not be tolerated today were then accepted as essential to success.

TRENDS IN THE QUALIFICATIONS CF THE EXECUTIVES

While wealth and family position have never been listed among the qualifications for top office, all the evidence points to the fact that the sons of wealthy families have a better chance of reaching the top executive position than those from poor or middle-income families. This is due in some measure to the greater opportunities for

[1] Quoted in A. A. Berle, Jr., *Studies in the Law of Corporation Finance*, Chicago: Callaghan, 1928, p. 1.

inheritance, and in a somewhat lesser degree to the possession of capital which makes it possible to "buy" control. The data on the way in which the individuals from families of different income levels reached the top make this clear. But those from higher income groups also have the advantages of more social contacts with influential businessmen and greater opportunities for higher education than those from relatively poor families. And even though they work their way to the top within the company, their chances of doing so are better if they have the advantages of wealth.

These advantages continue to be important in the large corporations, but they are declining in importance. The increase in size of the corporations has diminished the opportunities for controlling through investment. The growing diffusion of stockholdings means that fewer and fewer executives have any substantial investment in their own companies. And this same diffusion of stockholdings makes it necessary for directors to render a kind of public accounting for their acts. This, in turn, means that they must defend their choice of a chief executive. And it is probable that the succession of a son to his father's position requires rather special defense. Consequently, even when there are heirs who are interested and reasonably well qualified, they do not automatically succeed to the throne.

Another factor, partly related to the increasing size and age of the corporations, is the tendency to select individuals with both a college education and long experience with the company. This favors the heirs in some measure, but it also opens the way to others. A young man from a comparatively poor family, provided that he is able to make his way through college, can start at the bottom in a large corporation and eventually work his way to the top. He makes the necessary contacts with influential people on the job. Thus, while it is still true that the chances of reaching the top are very much smaller for those from low-income families than they are for those from high-income families, they are better than they used to be. The decline in the proportion of executives from wealthy families is not to be accounted for by any corresponding decline in the proportion of wealthy families in the total population.

The poor boy has less chance of starting his own enterprise than he had fifty years ago. It takes more capital even for small enterprises, and also it is increasingly difficult for a small concern to compete with the giants already in the field. In the past, starting a new enterprise has been one important channel through which the poor boy with only a grammar school or at best a high school education could reach the top. But the virtual disappearance of this channel appears to have been more than compensated for by the increasing opportunity of getting the necessary college education in the first place, and then working up in the big corporation. A college degree has become more important than great wealth, and easier to obtain. The sons of families in the low-income groups will not reach the top as quickly as the sons of the wealthy, but the chance of arriving eventually is improving. This is important because it means that the chance of those from low-income families reaching high position is, if anything, better than earlier, and social mobility has to that extent increased. It is important also because it means that the selection of the top executives is made from a widening circle, and to that degree the chance of getting the best talent is increased.[2]

The data of this study show that the proportion of executives with higher education has not only increased over the period studied; it has increased out of proportion to the increase in college graduates among the male population as a whole. For the 1950 group the proportion of college-educated among executives was about twelve times that for the entire male population of their age group. It has not yet reached the proportion of college-trained individuals found among the distinguished individuals included in Who's Who in America, but the lag of business leaders behind other distinguished individuals with respect to education is less for the 1950 group than for the preceding generation of business leaders. The point will soon be reached when a college degree is a prerequisite to promotion to the top position.

This requirement is not as serious a barrier to the success of those

[2] To the extent that there is discrimination at the bottom, however, talent and a college education will not prove sufficient. Poverty as such does not appear to disqualify a college graduate, but the "wrong" race, nationality, or religion may. Insofar as this occurs, the group from which the chief executives are eventually chosen is needlessly restricted.

from middle-income and low-income families as it might have been fifty years ago. There are more state and municipal universities than formerly, and while even for these tuition has tended to increase, they are more accessible geographically, and scholarship aid in some measure offsets increased tuition. Most of the 1950 executives, of course, obtained their education twenty-five years or more ago, when tuition was lower.

Another factor which helps to open the road to success to the low-income groups is the increasing age of required school attendance, combined with the prohibition of child labor. Poor boys no longer go to work at the age of nine or ten to help support a widowed mother. They will continue their schooling even if it means that their mothers have to go to work or apply for aid to dependent children. This results in an increasing number of individuals obtaining the educational prerequisite to college. The proportion of boys graduating from high school increased ninefold between the generation represented by the 1900 executives and that represented by the 1950 executives. The majority of boys of college age today have completed a high school education. And once the preparatory education is completed, the next step is easier and more likely to be taken.

What *kind* of education makes for a successful executive is less clear. The desirability of a general rather than a specialized education is often stressed, but the proportion of those with specialized degrees is very high and rising. There is some evidence that this increase is due to the fact that the specialists are chosen in the first place for specialized jobs quite unrelated to administration and that the growing policy of selecting executives from within the company leads to a predominance of specialists among the second-ranking officers from whom the chief is eventually chosen. Training for general administration is rare, and the demand for "general administrators" just out of college is almost unheard of. It is engineers and physicists, accountants and lawyers, that are sought at that level.

The comparison of the executives of fast-growing and static corporations suggests that college education contributes to success but not specialized education in such fields as law and engineering. However, the data on which this comparison is based are too limited to be regarded as proof of this. Whether the executives of the fast-growing corporations specialized in business courses in their undergraduate training to a greater or lesser degree than those from the static corporations is not known.

The most dramatic shift in business experience between the older and younger generations of this study is in the proportion that have had independent business experience at some time in their careers. Two-thirds of the early appointees among the 1900 executives were at some time in their lives running their own business enterprise, large or small. For the more recent appointees among the 1950 executives, on the contrary, only 11 percent had ever had such experience. There is some increase among the current executives in the number with specialized professional training, but the great increase is in the number of business administrators. More than this, the proportion whose entire business career has been limited to the company they head has increased from 7 percent for the 1900 executives to 22 percent for the 1950 executives. Not only are they specialists in their education: with increasing frequency they also are specialists in a single business organization. And the majority of those with other business experience have spent the larger part of their business lives with the companies they head.

This inbreeding is not limited to the chief executives. It extends in some measure to the boards of directors themselves. The great majority of corporations in 1900 were controlled by boards in which outside directors were in the majority, and while this is still true for railroads and public utilities, among the industrials a majority of the boards have enough officers on them to account for half or more of the board. This development appears to be deplored both by the corporation officials and by authorities on administrative practice, but there is no sign of its being corrected. And there is some evidence, in spite of the arguments against this development, that the companies with largely inside boards not only do not use their power for their personal gains, as some have feared, but are operating more successful companies than the others.

THE 1950 EXECUTIVE—ACTUAL AND IDEAL

A "profile" of the chief executive of the large business corporation of 1950 is given below. The age and years of service ascribed to him are the median values for the 1950 group. The other attributes are modal values.

The typical executive of 1950 is a native American, the son of a small, independent business man. His family's income was moderate, and such jobs as he pursued during his boyhood were for extra spending money rather than to help support the family. His parents managed to put him through college, with such contributions as he himself made to his own expenses through part-time employment, mostly in summer. Upon graduation he obtained a full-time job, with no assistance from his family. Thenceforward he was on his own. While still relatively young and inexperienced he obtained a minor position with the corporation that he eventually headed, and he gradually worked up, through operations or production, to a vice presidency, from which he was promoted to the presidency at the age of fifty-two. Although he has had specialized professional training, he has never practiced independently, nor has he at any time run a business of his own as his father did. He is a business administrator —a bureaucrat—with little job experience outside his own corporation. His investments in "his" company are nominal, in terms of potential control—less than 0.1 percent of the total stock outstanding. He is a Republican in politics; he attends the Episcopalian church, if he attends church at all; and he served the federal government in an advisory capacity during the war. He was, in 1950, sixty-one years of age, and he will probably be seventy when he retires.

This profile differs markedly from that of an "ideal" executive. The top position in the big corporation is attractive enough to command the best talent. But the extent of the search for talent leaves something to be desired since more often than not it is limited to the officers of the corporation itself. And even within the corporation what guarantee is there that the man selected was the best the organization could produce and not just an able but chance favorite of the outgoing executive? The ideal executive would be selected from a wider circle. Today's executive is less likely, however, to inherit or buy his office than the executive of fifty years ago, and to that extent he is more likely to be chosen on merit than his predecessors.

Another deviation of today's executive from the ideal is in the breadth of his training. He is first a specialist in engineering, or the law, or some other field unrelated to the job of administration. And second, most if not all of his working life has been limited to a single corporation. These limitations do not preclude breadth of vision and understanding, but is this kind of training likely to be as useful an experience as running one's own business or serving as the top administrator of another, smaller corporation, where he has had to make decisions and take the responsibility for them to an extent rarely permitted among junior executives? The self-appointed executives of 1900 who had built up their own enterprises had usually demonstrated their ability by the fact that their enterprises had survived.

A third shortcoming of today's executives is the age at which they "arrive." Too many are appointed at an age that will not permit any extended period of administration before they must retire. The ten-year span before 65 which some of the authorities set up as a minimum reasonable term of office simply is not realized in the majority of cases.

This raises the question whether these shortcomings are important, or whether the "ideal" is in fact not the best type for a chief executive. The only evidence that this study offers on this question is the comparison between the executives of the fast-growing and the static companies. If it is assumed that the fast-growing companies are the more successful group and that the executives of the fast-growing companies are responsible in some measure for their success, then the evidence supports the assumption that the qualifications of the typical executive are not the best. The executives of the fast-growing corporations came closer to the ideal than those of the static companies in several respects. They reached the top at forty-nine, on the average—five years younger than the executives of the static companies. Also their service with the corporation they headed averaged eight years less before they were promoted than the service of the other group of executives. They had a more varied business experience before joining their company, and they had had a less specialized education to begin with—less engineering and less law. Also, a larger proportion of them had had experience as independent businessmen.

Why, then, do the corporations promote from within so frequently? And why do they promote so late? The reasons appear to be first, that the talent within the company is better known, and to that extent safer, than outside talent. Also, there is always a feeling that one's own company is different and that intimate knowledge of its problems is important from the start. The president or chairman is likely to select his successor in advance and to groom him personally for the job. And loyalty to the company is stressed. Moreover, there is a sense of obligation to the officers with whom the chief has worked, and a conviction—which is doubtless justified—that morale will be higher and the chance of retaining able executives greater, if they are aware that the top offices will be filled from within. And finally, the man who has served long and successfully in a vice presidential capacity may be felt to deserve the recognition of top office, even though he is admittedly too old when the vacancy occurs. On the other hand, there have been some important gains from the professionalization of business administration.

PROFESSIONALIZATION OF LEADERSHIP

The fact that professionalization of leadership is occurring is evidenced by various changes. The first is the greater degree of education required for executives, even though the kind of education is not as clearly defined as it is for such professions as law, medicine, and engineering. The graduate school of business administration is too recent a phenomenon for its graduates to have played any important role among the executives at mid-century, but in another generation it should be possible to judge better whether graduate degrees in this field are to become increasingly important as a way of getting to the top.

A second test of professionalization is the fact that, given a higher education, the man from a low-income family appears to have a better chance of reaching the top than he had fifty years ago. It is less and less possible either to inherit the top position or to buy it. Two-thirds of the 1950 executives were chosen for administrative success either in their own companies or in others. Their promotion came as a result of merit rather than family influence or financial backing.

A third test of professionalization is the development of a code of ethics. This factor is not included in the data of this study, owing to its intangible nature. But any careful reading of the speeches and writings of the executives themselves as well as of the writings of students in this field makes it very clear that many practices that were entirely acceptable fifty years ago are no longer tolerated. And while here, as elsewhere, the standard has been imposed in part by law and is by no means universally accepted, many of the more articulate business leaders are subscribing to ethical standards that go far beyond any legal requirements. And this code of ethics more and more recognizes the public interest and places the public good ahead of private gain. As yet this code of fair practices has not been spelled out in the same measure as the codes of the older professions, and is not completely recognized by most of the big business executives. But it does exist.

The final test of professionalization is the long period of apprenticeship and the gradual rise to the top. Almost universally the chief executive has had long experience in administration in second-ranking offices, and more and more there is an effort to train the most promising of the younger executives on the job, with higher office in view.

This professionalization of leadership is deplored by many who fear that it might result in killing innovation and risk taking; that big business might settle into well-worn grooves, and change and progress be stifled. But if the performance of big business in recent years is taken as a test of the ability of these leaders, they must be judged successful. Any loss in imagination and daring appears to be offset by a more scientific approach to the problems of production and by more planning and research. Also, it is always possible that some detachment from the profit motive may encourage risk taking, within limits—a calculated risk rather than a hunch. Detachment from immediate profit may also make the leaders more ready to consider the claims of labor, of the consumer, and even of that hard-to-define group, the general public. In short, it may result in maximization of production rather than profits. This end may well be fostered, also, by the engineers, trained in efficiency and quantity production, and by the decline of the financiers seeking profits through the "conscientious withdrawal of efficiency," to use Veblen's terminology.

Finally, the division of powers among several executives, and perhaps an entire board of directors composed of full-time employees, means that with greater frequency important decisions will be the considered judgment of a well-informed group of men rather than the decision of an individual, rubber-stamped by an outside board with too many other interests and responsibilities to be fully informed. But while these gains are very real, it seems probable that even better leadership could be achieved. There is still much to be learned about the kind of university education that is best suited to developing the executive of the future. And the search for qualified executives should probably be widened, with more stress on a wider business experience, and also with insistence on promotion at a somewhat younger age. The search for talent at the lower levels, also, is probably too limited. It is usually limited, in the first place, to specialists in a few fields, not necessarily the most relevant for general administration. And, in the second place, there is sometimes discrimination against minority groups.

With the decline in competition, other measures must be taken if the ablest executives are to find their way to the top positions. And the process of professionalization appears to be the route by which this is most likely to be achieved. Business administration still has a long way to go before it can be accepted as a profession in its own right. To date, most of the professional training and most of the professional standards found among the executives have been borrowed from other professions. Perhaps these will do, but it seems probable that the graduate schools of business administration will succeed in the end in setting up more appropriate standards. And to the extent that professionalization of business administration is achieved, it may serve as an increasingly important factor in modifying the anti-social tendencies of big business that made "trust busting" a popular political issue in the earlier history of business combinations.

BIBLIOGRAPHY

Abrams, F. W. "Management's Responsibilities in a Complex World," *Harvard Business Review*, XXIX, No. 3 (May, 1951), 29–34.

Adams, Stuart. "Trends in Occupational Origins of Business Leaders," *American Sociological Review*, XIX, No. 5 (October, 1954), 541–48.

Allen, F. L. The Big Change. New York: Harper, 1952.

Baker, J. C. Directors and Their Functions. Boston: Harvard Graduate School of Business Administration, 1945.

Barnard, C. I. The Functions of the Executive. Cambridge: Harvard University Press, 1948.

Barron, C. W. They Told Barron. New York: Harper, 1930.

Berle, A. A., Jr. Studies in the Law of Corporation Finance. Chicago: Callaghan, 1928.

——— The Twentieth Century Capitalist Revolution. New York: Harcourt Brace, 1954.

Berle, A. A., Jr., and G. C. Means. The Modern Corporation and Private Property. New York: Commerce Clearing House, 1932.

Cherne, Leo. "Harry A. Bullis," *Saturday Review*, XXXVII (January 23, 1954), 24–25.

Clarkson Letter, The (January, 1954).

Clews, Henry. Fifty Years in Wall Street. New York: Irving, 1908.

Cochran, T. C. Railroad Leaders, 1845–1890. Cambridge: Harvard University Press, 1953.

Collier, A. T. "Business Leadership and a Creative Society," *Harvard Business Review*, XXXI, No. 1 (January–February, 1953), 29–38.

Corporate Director, The (November, 1950): "More Facts About Presidents."

Coyle, David C. "Movie Mogul, $800,000—Truman, $100,000," *New York Times Magazine* (January 30, 1949), pp. 5ff.

Destler, C. M. "Entrepreneurial Leadership Among the 'Robber Barons,'" *Journal of Economic History*, Supplement VI (1946), 28–49.

Dimock, M. E., and H. K. Hyde. "Executive Appointment in Private and Public Bureaucracies," in R. K. Merton and others, Reader in Bureaucracy. Glencoe: Free Press, 1952. Pages 319–27.

Drucker, P. F. The New Society. Harper: New York, 1950.

Forbes, B. C. America's Fifty Foremost Business Leaders. New York: B. C. Forbes, 1948.

Fortune, XXXIII, No. 4 (April, 1941), 61ff.: "Bethlehem Steel"; XLVI, No. 5 (November, 1952), 132ff.: "The Nine Hundred"; XLVII, No. 4 (April, 1953), 113–14: "Should a Business Man Be Educated?"

Galbraith, J. K. American Capitalism. Boston: Houghton Mifflin, 1952.

Gerstenberg, C. W. Financial Organization and Management of Business. New York: Prentice Hall, 1939.

Gilbert, Lewis D. "Management and the Public Stockholder," *Harvard Business Review,* XXVIII, No. 4 (July, 1950), 73–83.

Gordon, R. A. Business Leadership in the Large Corporation. Washington: Brookings, 1945.

Greenewalt, C. H. "We're Going to Need More Executives." Speech before the Executives Club of Chicago, May 1, 1953.

Holbrook, S. H. The Age of the Moguls. New York: Doubleday, 1953.

Janney, J. E. "Company Presidents Look at Themselves," *Harvard Business Review,* XXX, No. 3 (May–June, 1952), 59–70.

Jenks, L. H. "Role Structure of Entrepreneurial Personality," in Change and the Entrepreneur. Cambridge: Harvard University Press, 1949. Pages 108–52.

Keller, Suzanne I. "The Social Origins and Career Lines of Three Generations of American Business Leaders." New York: Columbia University, unpublished Ph.D. thesis, 1953.

McMurry, R. N. "Man-Hunt for Top Executives," *Harvard Business Review,* XXXII, No. 1 (January–February, 1954), 46–62.

Marshall, Alfred. Principles of Economics. 8th ed. London: Macmillan, 1946.

Miller, William. "American Historians and the Business Elite," *Journal of Economic History,* IX, No. 2 (November, 1949), 184–208.

Miller, William, ed. Men in Business. Cambridge: Harvard University Press, 1952.

Mills, C. Wright. "The American Business Elite: A Collective Portrait," *Journal of Economic History,* Supplement V (1945), 20–44.

Moody, John. The Truth About the Trusts. New York: Moody, 1904.

National Industrial Conference Board. "The Corporate Directorship." Studies in Business Policy, No. 63 (1953).

—— "Executive Expense Accounts." Studies in Business Policy, No. 67 (1954).

Newcomer, Mabel. "The Chief Executives of Large Business Corporations," in Vol. V of Explorations in Entrepreneurial History. Harvard University, 1952–53. Pages 1–33.

Norton-Taylor, Duncan. "The Business Schools: Pass or Flunk," *Fortune,* XLIX, No. 6 (June, 1954), 112ff.

Prentis, H. W., Jr. "Liberal Education for Business and Industry, *Bulletin of the American Association of University Professors,* XXXVIII, No. 3 (Autumn, 1952), 345–55.

Quinn, T. K. Giant Business. New York: Exposition Press, 1953.

Stryker, Perrin. "Do Stock Options Pay?" *Fortune,* L, No. 6 (December, 1954), 118ff.

Suman, John R. "Growing a Good Executive Crop." New York: Standard Oil Co. of N.J., pamphlet, 1954.

Swope, Gerard. "Some Aspects of Corporate Management," *Harvard Business Review,* XXIII, No. 3 (Spring, 1945), 314–22.

Taussig, F. W., and C. S. Joslyn. American Business Leaders. New York: Macmillan, 1932.

Thompson, C. D. Confessions of the Power Trust. New York: Dutton, 1932.

Wald, R. M., and R. A. Doty. "The Top Executives—a Firsthand Profile," *Harvard Business Review,* XXXII, No. 4 (July–August, 1954), 45–54.

Weinberg, S. J. "A Corporation Director Looks at His Job," *Harvard Business Review,* XXVII, No. 5 (September, 1949), 585–93.

Whyte, William H., Jr. "How Hard Do Executives Work?" *Fortune,* XLIX, No. 1 (January, 1954), 108ff.

——— Is Anybody Listening? New York: Simon & Schuster, 1952.

INDEX

Abilities: required, in executive officer, 20, 21-22, 41, 134, 135; *see also* Qualifications

Abrams, F. W., 136; quoted, 20

Accountants, 132, 147

Administrators, salaried, 5, 90-93, 127

Advertising, 107, 108

Ages, of executive officers, 17; relation to family status and education, 64, 78-79; at time of first position, 87-89; when attaining office, 111-12, 138-39, 150; at termination of office, 117-20; at retirement, 149

Agreements, to limit competition, 37-38

Air lines, 11; *see also* Industrial corporations

Alcoa, 116

Allen, F. L., quoted, 21, 23

Amalgamated Copper, 44

American Agricultural Chemical, 66

American Business Leaders (Taussig and Joslyn), 12n, 52, 56, 70, 71

American Can Company, 44, 134

American Hide and Leather, 88

American Railway Express, 44

American Smelting and Refining Company, 30

American Telephone and Telegraph, 128

American Tobacco Company, 36

American Woolen, 6

Amherst, 74

Antitrust legislation, *see* Government regulation

Apprenticeship, 152

Armstrong Cork, 66

Assistants, to chief executive officer, 20-21

Assman, Franz A., 44, 45n

Atlantic Refinery, 135

Australia, 43

Authority, distribution of, 142-43

Avery, Sewell, 23

Bankers, 61, 90, 136; on boards of directors, 32-35, 40

Baptists, 46-48

Barnard, C. I., 21; quoted, 22

Barron, C. W., 66

Behn, Sosthenes, 42, 43

Berle, A. A., Jr., 144

Berle and Means, 5

Bethlehem Steel, 31, 36, 38, 126, 129

Big business, public attitudes toward, 10; growth of, 13

Board chairman, *see* Chairman of board of directors

Board of directors: public on, 6; questions about, 17; relations of, with executive officer, 19, 23-26, 28, 29, 109; size of, 24-25; powers and responsibilities of, 24, 29, 143; composition of, 25-40; dummy, 31; salaries, 31, 127; relation to company's growth, 32; comparison of boards of different periods, 40; *see also* Insiders, on boards of directors; Outsiders, on boards of directors

Bolivia, 42

Bonus, 122, 126

Bookkeepers, 108

Bradley, Robert S., quoted, 66

Brady, Anthony, 45n

Brooklyn, N.Y., 50

Brooklyn Union Gas Company, 50

Bullis, Harry A., quoted, 66-67

Bureau of Labor Statistics, 11

Business administration programs, 65, 67-69, 74-75, 136, 151

Businessmen, independent, 53-59, 92-97, 148

Business Week, quoted, 141

Cabinet, 131

California, 122

California, University of, 74

Callaway, S. R., 45n

Canada, 43

Canadians, 42

Capitalists, 61, 89, 90, 92

"Career men," 4

Carlton, Albert, 50

Carnegie, Andrew, quoted, 41, 43-44, 131

Central of Georgia, 120

Chairman of board of directors: and president, 13-16, 22-26, 123-25; as chief executive officer, 14-15, 22, 113; *see also* Executive officers

Chance, 9, 130, 149